ccess Your Online Resources

rd Aware 1 is accompanied by a number of printable online materials, designed to ensure this ource best supports your professional needs

ivate your online resources:

to www.routledge.com/cw/speechmark and click on the cover of this book

ck the 'Sign in or Request Access' button and follow the instructions in order to access the resources

Throughout the book you will see this symbol whenever there are downloadable resources available on the companion website.

Now in a fully updated second edition, this comprehensive and practical book outlines the theoretical underpinnings for vocabulary and acts as a 'how to' guide to developing word learning across the school and curriculum. It is packed with easy-to-implement activities, worksheets and resources that can be put into practice immediately with individual students or groups, whole classes and throughout the school.

The *Word Aware* approach provides a structured framework to promote vocabulary development in all children and has been rigorously tried and tested. Now in full colour, with photocopiable and downloadable materials, it is an outstanding resource that will be an essential addition to any school and classroom.

The second edition of *Word Aware 1* brings:

- An even wider range of ready-to-go vocabulary activities
- Fine-tuned teaching techniques
- Enhanced resources to develop children's independent word learning skills
- A step-by-step guide to developing a whole school approach

Word Aware 1 is an invaluable tool for teachers and other professionals looking to support children as they broaden their vocabulary. It is particularly suited to children aged 5–11 years but can easily be adapted for older children.

Stephen Parsons is a Speech and Language Therapist, trainer and author of practical language development resources for teachers and Speech and Language Therapists (SaLTs). From 1996–2017, Stephen worked as a Speech and Language Therapy Service Manager in Hackney and the City of London. With over 30 years' experience in the field, he is co-author of bestselling Speechmark resources *Language for Thinking* (second edition, 2017), *Word Aware* (first edition, 2013), *Word Aware 2* (2017) and *Language for Behaviour and Emotions* (2020). Stephen graduated in Speech Pathology from Flinders University, before attaining an MSc in Speech and Language Therapy from City University in 2000. He currently serves as Chair of NAPLIC, the association for professionals working with children and young people with developmental language disorder.

Anna Branagan is a Speech and Language Therapist. In Gloucestershire, Anna works within a Youth Support Team supporting vulnerable young people. In Worcestershire, she works within mainstream schools supporting inclusive practice. Anna trained at Leeds Metropolitan University 25 years ago. She is the co-author of bestselling Speechmark resources *Language for Thinking* (second edition, 2017), *Word Aware* (first edition, 2013), *Word Aware 2* (2017) and *Language for Behaviour and Emotions* (2020).

Teaching Vocabulary Across the Day, Across the Curriculum

Second Edition

Stephen Parsons and Anna Branagan

Routledge
Taylor & Francis Group

LONDON AND NEW YORK

Second edition published 2022
by Routledge
2 Park Square, Milton Park, Abingdon, Oxon, OX14 4RN

and by Routledge
605 Third Avenue, New York, NY 10158

Routledge is an imprint of the Taylor & Francis Group, an informa business

© 2022 Stephen Parsons and Anna Branagan

First edition published by Speechmark 2013

British Library Cataloguing-in-Publication Data
A catalogue record for this book is available from the British Library

Library of Congress Cataloging-in-Publication Data
Names: Branagan, Anna, author. | Parsons, Stephen (Speech therapist) author.
Title: Word aware : teaching vocabulary across the day, across the
    curriculum / Anna Branagan and Stephen Parsons.
Description: Second edition. | Abingdon, Oxon ; New York, NY : Routledge,
    2021. | Includes bibliographical references.
Identifiers: LCCN 2020042535 (print) | LCCN 2020042536 (ebook) | ISBN 9780367675028 (hardback) |
    ISBN 9780367462659 (paperback) | ISBN 9781003027812 (ebook)
Subjects: LCSH: Vocabulary--Study and teaching (Elementary) | Language arts
    (Elementary) | Education, Elementary--Curricula.
Classification: LCC LB1574.5 .B68 2021 (print) | LCC LB1574.5 (ebook) |
    DDC 372.44--dc23
LC record available at https://lccn.loc.gov/2020042535
LC ebook record available at https://lccn.loc.gov/2020042536

ISBN: 978-0-367-67502-8 (hbk)
ISBN: 978-0-367-46265-9 (pbk)
ISBN: 978-1-003-02781-2 (ebk)

Typeset in Berthold Akzidenz Grotesk
by Apex CoVantage, LLC

Visit the companion website: www.routledge.com/cw/speechmark

Contents

Foreword

In the seven years since we wrote the first edition of *Word Aware: Teaching Vocabulary Across the Day, Across the Curriculum* there has been a great upsurge in interest in vocabulary within the education sector. Many teachers privately knew that vocabulary was important, but this was not reflected in curriculum guidance. Introduction of the Common Core Standards in the United States (corestandards.org) and the new National Curriculum in England (gov.uk/government/collections/national-curriculum), among others have both given greater prominence to vocabulary, but often little guidance as to 'how'. There is also greater awareness that our classrooms include a large number of learners for whom vocabulary is a barrier to learning, and that the best place to support them is in the classroom.

Over the past seven years we have visited many schools and had a great number of conversations with a wide range of educators about vocabulary. The enthusiasm with which *Word Aware* has been received has driven us forward to build the approach and make it even better. Our key aim is to bring research and best practice together and create a vocabulary teaching method which is straightforward to implement and effective.

This book provides:

- A structured framework to support all children's word learning.
- An easy-to-implement, step-by-step guide for developing whole school practice.
- Downloadable and photocopiable resources that you can use right away.
- Fun and creative ideas to inspire you and your class, and keep vocabulary learning fresh.
- An evidence-informed approach underpinned by theory and research.

We are always keen to hear from practitioners, to hear about successes, answer queries, support research and share our love of words. Contact us via thinkingtalking.co.uk or on Twitter @WordAware (Stephen), @Lang4Think (Anna).

Stephen Parsons and Anna Branagan

Acknowledgements

Thanks to Kevin, Steve, Toby and Lily for all your support and tolerance.

1. Introduction

Vocabulary is Important

It is hard to overstate the importance of vocabulary. In our daily lives a well-chosen word will often help us to connect with others and deepen understanding, or alternatively defuse a tense situation. The spoken and written word can also be used to entertain in the form of jokes, novels and playscripts. Our media may be more visually based than in the past, but the finer points are still reliant on words. Advancements in science are built upon the exchange of ideas, which is primarily done by words. Our democracies are based on words, as words are used to debate issues and the resultant laws are recorded in words. Our society and our culture are built upon words, and so those with greater verbal and written abilities will have a greater chance of navigating life's complexities.

And nowhere are words more important than in our schools. Vocabulary impacts on the curriculum, because to comprehend what we read, to master mathematics or to make sense of science, we must first understand the words and what they mean. This is being increasingly recognised internationally and vocabulary given a higher profile in various curricula such as the Common Core in the Unites States and the English National Curriculum which states 'Pupils' acquisition and command of vocabulary are key to their learning and progress across the whole curriculum. Teachers should therefore develop vocabulary actively, building systematically on pupils' current knowledge' (2014).

Vocabulary Impacts

Vocabulary impacts on reading. A child who knows lots of spoken words is better equipped to master reading and, as Wegener and Castles (2018) state, 'when children see a written word for the first time, they are more likely to read it correctly if they have heard it before'. Hjetland et al. (2017), in their systematic review, found vocabulary to be a predictive factor in children's later reading development. Spencer et al. (2019) sampled 400,000 children and of the weak readers only 0.01% had typically developing vocabulary (which they defined as above the 25th centile).

Vocabulary also impacts right across the curriculum; as Riccomini et al. (2015) state, 'rich development and understanding of mathematics vocabulary is essential for students to become actively engaged in mathematics past mundane computational requirements to thorough understanding and meaning making'. The average person in the street may think that mathematics is about addition, subtraction and times tables, without understanding it involves high levels of abstract vocabulary. As the Department for Education (DfE, England) found, those with poor spoken language skills (including vocabulary) are at great risk in literacy but even greater risk in mathematics: 'Children who are behind in language development at age five are six times less likely to reach the expected standard in English at age eleven, and 11 times less likely to achieve the expected level in maths' (DfE, 2017).

Vocabulary continues to impact right through life and Law et al. (2009) found that children with poor vocabulary at 5 years of age had worse outcomes than typically developing peers at 34 years across a range of life measures including education, employment and mental health after controlling for socio-economic status and family factors. According to the English school inspectorate, Ofsted (2019), 'the correlation between vocabulary size and life chances is as firm as any correlation in educational research. Vocabulary is important because it embodies and communicates concepts.'

Vocabulary Gap

In recent years there has been an upsurge in the interest in vocabulary. In a recent survey (OUP, 2018) 69% of the primary school teachers said 'that they think the number of pupils with limited vocabulary is either increasing or significantly increasing in their schools compared to a few years ago'. The same survey found that, according to teacher reports, on average 49% of Year 1 pupils have a limited vocabulary to the extent that it affects their learning (OUP, 2018).

This greater awareness has led to concern for the so-called 'vocabulary gap' (Quigley, 2018) between those with well-developed vocabularies and their less advanced peers. Waldfogel and Washbrook, (2010) found that this gap is linked to poverty, with a 20 month gap at age 5 years between the wealthiest and the poorest. According to Biemiller's (2005) report, the gap has grown so that, 'by the end of second grade, disadvantaged students can lag two years behind the average students in their class and four years behind students in the upper quartile'. The gap continues to grow and as Ford-Connors and Paratore (2015) highlight, 'students who enter classrooms with a low store of vocabulary knowledge are unlikely to acquire complex knowledge through simple exposure'.

Addressing Vocabulary

There is wide recognition that vocabulary needs to be addressed, including researchers such as Spencer et al. (2017), who state, 'language skills, and in particular vocabulary skills, may play a key role in the continuing drive to reduce the gap in educational attainment between groups from differing socio-economic backgrounds'.

A widely reported estimate is that an average adult has 30,000 words in their vocabulary (Clark, 1993), and some other estimates are as high as 50,000 words for an average adult. To achieve even the lower figure, a child must learn approximately six to eight words per day throughout their years at school. A child who starts school with fewer words than their peers will need to learn at a significantly faster rate if they are to reach the average adult target. They may make good progress in one year with a teacher who focuses on vocabulary, but this will not be enough. To have a chance of closing the gap and achieving an average-sized vocabulary, they will need to learn words at an accelerated rate over a number of years. This herculean task can only be achieved by a consistent approach across the school that is sustained over a number of years by all involved: teachers, support staff, families and, of course, the child.

Wright (2012) observed teachers talking about vocabulary with their students. On average there were eight vocabulary-related conversations per day, but the number varied from 0 to 20 times. Teachers rarely spoke about the same word twice on the same day. On average, teachers used 2.5 utterances per target word. We know from others' research (Stahl & Nagy, 2005) that children need at least 12 exposures to a word to learn it, so leaving vocabulary to casual instruction will not be sufficient.

In more recent years there is a growing consensus around what good vocabulary instruction should consist of. It is perhaps best summarised by Graves (2015) as a rich language environment, direct teaching of word meanings, strategy instruction, and supporting students' word consciousness (i.e.: awareness that words are important). Wasik et al., 2016 concur that 'optimally effective vocabulary interventions will offer children systematic exposures to words, as well as opportunities for a range of active-processing tasks'. After reviewing the literature, the Educational Endowment Foundation came to the conclusion that approaches which aim to improve spoken vocabulary 'work best when they are related to current content being studied in school, and when they involve active and meaningful use of any new vocabulary' (2019).

Vocabulary is for Everyone

Children will have different home experiences (Hart and Risley, 1995) and also different word learning needs as a result of conditions such as Developmental Language Disorder. Children with English as an additional language (English language learners) will also bring their own vocabulary experiences and innate word learning abilities, as well as facing the hurdle of learning words in school in a language that differs from the one used at home. An inclusive and adaptable approach to word learning is therefore necessary so that the needs of all word learners can be met.

Vocabulary Outcomes and Considerations

There are a growing number of studies of the impacts of vocabulary interventions and their impact on reading. A general summary is that there is often a significant impact on the words which have been taught but little impact on standardised assessments of reading comprehension (Elleman et al 2009). This may be because most interventions are relatively short-term and so are unable to teach enough words to make an impact on the number of words students are likely to encounter when reading. At first impression this is disheartening news, but it also emphasises the need for interventions which run across years, as well as multi-faceted programmes which address vocabulary from a number of different perspectives.

Vocabulary Programmes

Word Aware applies the above theory to a practical and structured approach that can be used across all parts of the curriculum. It can be used effectively by individual practitioners. However, *Word Aware* will have the most long-term effect on word learning if it is adopted by the whole school so that all involved develop a common understanding and apply a consistent approach.

This resource has been developed from classroom practice in conjunction with wide-ranging reading. The second edition has been refined as a result of advances in understanding and feedback from practitioners. We continue to build on these techniques for vocabulary teaching and in particular investigate the effectiveness of these methods. We would appreciate hearing your experiences and can be contacted via www.thinkingtalking.co.uk

Key Principles of Effective Vocabulary Teaching

The *Word Aware* principles have been developed by reviewing the literature and applying these concepts in the classroom. The authors have trained and worked with thousands of schools, teachers and educational practitioners over a number of years and refined the approach so that, while having a basis in theory, it makes sense in the classroom. These principles form the basis of the approach that is outlined in later sections.

The overarching principle is that all children will benefit if they:

- are exposed to enriched vocabulary within an environment where the spoken and written word are appreciated
- have opportunities to enjoy words
- experience explicit teaching of useful words
- learn strategies for independent word learning

Principle 1: A whole school approach

- Involve everyone across the school
- Teach vocabulary across all ages and all subjects

It is estimated that the average child learns 2,000–3,000 words per year, every year throughout their school years (Clark, 1993). This equates to six to eight words per day on average. While many of these words will be learnt without specific teaching, the sheer enormity of the task underlines that this is a process that must be continued across a number of years.

For a child with weaker vocabulary skills, a reasonable target might be to develop their vocabulary so it progresses from below average (say 20th centile) to average (50th centile). To meet this target, the child's rate of learning needs to increase from seven words per day to ten words per day, and to be sustained at this level for three years (Stahl & Nagy, 2005). No matter how effective, one teacher in one year or a short intervention will not be enough to make a difference. Instead a sustained day on day, year on year, whole school approach is required.

While the specific techniques will change as children move through the school, there needs to be a consistent commitment to the principles and their application.

Principle 2: Multifaceted approach

- Multi-sensory learning
- Integrated into every aspect of learning
- Vary approach to meet needs of learners

Graves (2015), among others, has called for multifaceted vocabulary intervention approaches. This makes sense because words are in every part of the curriculum (and lives) and they reflect children's experiences, so learning about words as part of, say, literacy can never be enough. Vocabulary teaching cannot sit within one curriculum area or be one person's responsibility. Vocabulary cannot be 'fixed' by taking one single action. Vocabulary teaching needs to be integrated into every aspect of learning.

Word learning is a long-term process and the words we will be teaching, and the skills of the learners, will change over time. Young learners need play-based activities, whilst older students can use words to talk about words (metalinguistics). A flexible and diverse approach will also engage the widest possible range of word learners. The risk is that if we rely solely on words to teach words then our most vulnerable learners will be less able to access the teaching.

One way to address this is to make use of the senses when teaching new words. Words will have more impact on learners if the senses are engaged. Experiencing how to 'saunter' means more than being told it is 'walking in a leisurely manner'. Being told that 'lustrous' means 'giving off light' does not have the same impact as seeing items such as lustrous hair, silk or metals.

Principle 3: Explicitly teach words

- Teach important words
- Breadth and depth

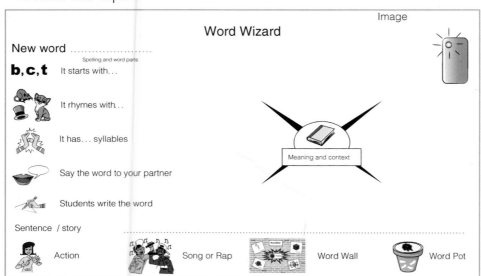

A printable colour version is available on the companion website.

An often-held premise is that exposing children to a language-rich learning environment is enough to promote vocabulary development. This may be enough for those students with good vocabulary learning skills, but for their peers with poor vocabulary, simple exposure is not enough (Ford-Connors and Paratore, 2015).

Word learning strategies are an important component of a vocabulary programme, but on their own they will also have limited impact. This is because to work out what a word means the reader needs to have a deep understanding of the text, which is a skill many with poor vocabulary often lack. Those with poor vocabulary are caught in a double bind, as they cannot make use of the rich language environment or word learning strategies.

Explicit teaching is therefore an essential component of a vocabulary programme. However, as there are so many words to learn, it cannot be the sole focus. In addition, the whole school day cannot be devoted to vocabulary so teaching time must be used judiciously. Care must be taken to select words that will have a direct impact on accessing learning as well as promoting literacy skills. The words should then be taught in a manner that impacts on all word learners, including the most vulnerable.

'Breadth' is used to refer to the number of words known, whereas 'depth' is how well a word is known. Both are important, but as there are so many words to learn and limited teaching time, there is a tension between the two. If students know lots of words but are not fully confident with their understanding, there is a risk they will either misuse them or not use them at all. It is a practitioner decision, but more important words need to be taught to greater depth so that they stick.

Principle 4: Use multiple exposures

- Children need to hear or read a new word many times
- They need opportunities to link new knowledge to what they already know

Most young children have well-developed word learning abilities and may form a tentative understanding after a small number of exposures (Rice et al., 1990). Research indicates that a child needs a minimum of 12 instructional encounters to establish simple understanding of a word (Stahl & Nagy, 2005). Exposures should be in a variety of contexts, so the child has the opportunity to build full comprehension (Block & Mangieri, 2006). Rather than learning definitions, children should hear the new word in real sentences that are related to situations with which they are familiar. For young children this may be about adults using the word while playing with the child, while for older pupils, meaningful exposures can be achieved by telling stories or talking about real events with which the class is familiar.

Word knowledge develops over time and initially a child will only have a vague understanding of a new word. However, as they hear the word in a variety of contexts, they will add new information and develop a richer and more complete understanding. Exposures may come from adults in school and at home, as well as from print and other media sources. Opportunities to use the word will further reinforce word knowledge as well as add to peers' learning.

Selecting words that will be encountered in other contexts such as at home, via media or in other subject areas will give the child opportunities to further develop their understanding of the word naturally. If, for

instance, 'volume' is introduced in science, the child may also encounter it in mathematics, when reading independently and on the side of a shampoo bottle at home, each time learning a little more about the word. If, however, a specific term like 'blotting paper' has been taught, the child is far less likely to encounter the word again and therefore will not have natural opportunities to expand their learning of the word. Exposures can, of course, be increased by directing children to read books on a topic or sending home 'talking homework' tasks that require parents and children to talk about the targeted word.

Principle 5: Teach words in context

- Provide practical learning opportunities
- Use the words in a variety of sentences

When a child first starts to learn the meaning of words, they do this by linking the language that they hear to the context around them. For instance, if a young child has a toy **bunny**, they are able to use their senses to explore the object. They touch its soft fur, they look at its pink eyes and maybe even taste its ear. When their parent labels the toy **bunny**, the child will over time link the word **bunny** to the toy. By learning all about **bunny** in a physical context the child has been able to establish its meaning.

The parent will also use a range of linguistic (language) contexts such as, 'He's a soft **bunny**', 'The **bunny** is jumping' and 'You're cuddling **bunny**'. By using a range of different sentences, the word **bunny** has also been placed in a linguistic context and the child will learn that it is a noun. The physical and linguistic contexts have both added to the development of a full understanding of the word. This is a natural process to which children are predisposed.

The example is for an early developing word, but the same principles apply as children get older. In the classroom it is possible to take advantage of children's natural word learning by giving them opportunities to explore new words in their physical context, because they will pick up more by using all five senses rather than just being instructed verbally. Learning about electrical circuits and how they work will have much more meaning if the word **circuit** is taught alongside a hands-on experiment. This is not always possible but learning opportunities can be enhanced by using pictures and simple apparatus.

Using the words in a range of meaningful sentences that relate to children's experiences gives the child a linguistic context. Giving examples of times when you would use the new word and thinking of times when children might use it will all add meaning. If you have more than one adult in the classroom, all should provide examples of the word in a sentence and when they might use the word. The differing examples will add to the richness of the instruction.

Principle 6: Link oral and written vocabulary

TRANSPARENT	Spoken vocabulary forms the basis for early reading development
The glass in the window is **transparent**	Reading exposes children to a rich and diverse vocabulary
Transparent	Spoken and written vocabularies support each other

Learning spoken words is something children are naturally able to do. When learning a spoken word, a child is able to gain clues from the speaker's voice and gesture, and to make full use of their senses: for instance, they can smell a pineapple or hear a bell. This kind of sensory information is not extractable from the page and thus gives the learning of oral vocabulary a natural advantage.

A strong foundation in oral language assists the transition to reading. If a child encounters a written word that is within their oral vocabulary, all they need to do is decode the word and they can understand it. If, however, the child encounters a word that is not in their oral vocabulary then they must first decode it, but then also decipher the meaning from the page. The page, even with a picture, provides far less information than spoken language. When reading, they will not be able to smell the sweetness of the pineapple nor hear the toll of the bell.

Books are a valuable source of words. The vocabulary used in books is far richer and more diverse than the vocabulary we use in our daily interactions. Hayes & Ahrens (1988) found that pre-school children's books contained a similar number of infrequently used or rare words as would be found in a conversation between college graduates. As children master reading, they are exposed to increasingly complex vocabulary and books become the prime source of new words. The biggest single factor that impacts on a child's long-term vocabulary development is their ability to read.

To have a fully developed understanding and mastery of a word we need to have the word established in both our spoken and written vocabularies (Nation, 1990). We need to be able to read it, write it and understand when we hear it, as well as speak it. If, for instance, we only ever read a word and never

say it or write it, we may struggle to pronounce it or later write it meaningfully in a sentence. By having multiple exposures to the word in both written and spoken contexts we have more chance of developing an in-depth understanding and subsequent ability to use it. By building opportunities within the classroom in which students are able to talk about words that they have read or to write words that they have heard, they will be able to make better connections between spoken and written language and thus develop a more robust vocabulary.

Principle 7: Analyse elements of the word

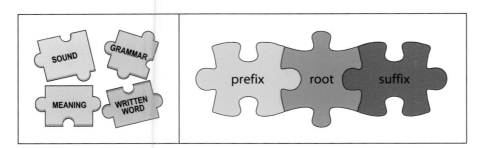

A young child learns to understand the words they hear around them by deciphering the speech sounds and attaching meaning to them. This is a natural process that all children are predisposed to do. The child is able to pick up clues from the speaker as well as take in information from what they see, hear, touch, smell and taste, and collate this to build up a meaning. By hearing the word in different contexts over time the child continues to add further information and develop a full understanding of the word (Chiat, 2000).

The child connects the phonological (speech sound), semantic (meaning) and grammatical elements together to form a representation of the word. Each word is connected into a network with other words. A word that the child is able to read and write will also need to integrate the grapheme (spelling) knowledge.

When words become more complex, there are also word parts (morphemes) to consider. There are prefixes at the start of words (such as 'mis-' in 'misunderstood') and suffixes at the end of words (such as '-ly' in 'cautiously') which are built onto root or base words and affect meaning.

Morphological analysis is noted as a key skill by a number of other researchers also. Nippold and Sun (2008) highlight that this skill becomes increasingly important from the top end of primary/elementary school onwards as words that children encounter become more morphologically complex. Sparks and Deacon (2015) found that vocabulary growth between Grades 2 and 3 was predicted by the children's skills with analysing morphology rather than the size of their vocabulary in Grade 2. Ford-Connors and Paratore (2015) conclude that 'morphological analysis provided a valuable tool to help students with and without disabilities to unlock word meanings. . . . students improved both knowledge of words and ability to infer meanings from new words'.

Teaching children phonic skills, talking about word meanings and prefixes and suffixes are tasks that teachers will do naturally, but by increasing children's awareness about the word learning process and strengthening their underlying skills it is possible to further improve their word learning skills.

Principle 8: Go with the child (at the right rate)

- Challenge but not overwhelm
- Ensure time for in-depth teaching

Selecting the right vocabulary is one of the most powerful tasks that a practitioner can undertake. It is important to select words that are at the right level and equate to Vygotsky's 'zone of proximal development' (Robson, 2006). Selecting words that are beyond the grasp of a child may lead to superficial knowledge, with the child being able to recite a definition but not being able to use the word meaningfully. While reinforcing existing words is important, selecting words that are too well-known is an inefficient use of time.

Similarly, the rate of vocabulary learning is also important. With so many words to learn and the general tempo of the curriculum there are inevitable time pressures. Despite this, it is important to allocate enough time to teach useful words to an appropriate depth (Stahl & Nagy, 2005; Beck et al., 2002). In-depth teaching will allow children to experience a number of meaningful exposures to the word and link the new word to existing knowledge and thus avoid superficial learning.

Also select texts that include appropriately challenging vocabulary: 'Children need reading texts that have an appropriate level of vocabulary so that they are not overwhelmed by a plethora of unknown words, but they also need to be challenged to learn (or refine) the meaning of words in the text.' (Oakhill et al., 2014)

Principle 9: Get excited about words

	• Build a word-rich environment
	• Celebrate words
	• Play word games

A word-enriched environment will expose children to wide and varied vocabulary and thus give them opportunities for incidental word learning. Building a word-enriched environment is not about one major

event, but rather involves many small actions. Selecting books or poetry for their use of vocabulary, high-lighting the use of words in texts and media, and commending students for their use of vocabulary will all contribute. Words can be given a higher profile by running whole class or whole school events, such as 'word of the week' awards.

One caveat is that the enriched vocabulary that children are exposed to still needs to be at an accessible level. Children need to be enthralled by words rather than overwhelmed by them.

Playing vocabulary games motivates word learners as well as providing them with opportunities to learn new words and reinforce known words. Most word games require the player to use phonologi-cal (speech sound) and semantic (meaning) skills. These are the same skills that are needed for word learning. Having fun with words is therefore important and should be a key component of any vocabulary intervention (Stahl & Nagy, 2005).

This skill is sometimes referred to as 'word consciousness' (Scott & Nagy, 2004) and in many ways forms the gateway to all word learning. For many word learners it increases their awareness and engagement with vocabulary, but also provides an opportunity to deepen their understanding by talking about words.

Principle 10: Teach strategies

- Children need to develop their own strategies
- Strategies are needed for spoken and written word learning

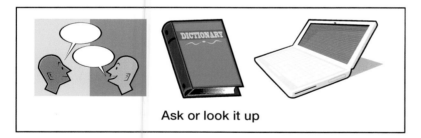

Ask or look it up

It is estimated that the average adult needs to have 30,000 words in her vocabulary and so it is not possible to teach every single word. Neither is it desirable. As children learn to read independently, an increasing number of new words are encountered via literature. Children will also be following their interests and so have an inclination to learn words that others may not be interested in. Having strate-gies to decipher the meaning of new words in both spoken and written form therefore becomes increas-ingly important for older children.

All children will benefit from being taught strategies that enhance their word learning (Nash & Snowling, 2006). Word learning strategies for younger children may be as simple as learning to ask, 'What does that word mean?' whereas for more advanced learners it may involve a number of strategies including morphology (word parts) and making use of contextual clues. Modelling word learning strategies is a powerful tool for all age groups and abilities.

Ford-Connors and Paratore (2015) highlight three key independent word learning strategies which impact on word learning: context clues, morphological analysis and polysemy (multiple meaning words) awareness. Nelson and Stage (2007) found that direct teaching of polysemous words had an effect, especially on children with weaker vocabulary and reading comprehension.

Whereas a great deal of focus is on deciphering the meanings of written words, it is important to also encourage students to ask others about the meaning of words that they hear. Children with less developed word learning skills may have a tendency not to ask about word meanings. Instilling a culture in the classroom that it is OK for children to ask if they do not know the meaning of a word is therefore an important step.

Principle 11: Work in partnership with families

- Get the whole family involved in word learning
- Support home language learning

This point may be last, but it definitely is not least. Vocabulary learning happens across the day and across contexts. To truly know a word a child must hear it and use it across contexts. At school there is less opportunity for one-to-one conversation, and although time is scarce at home as well, there is a greater chance for children to have the conversations which deepen understanding. At home children can also follow their own interests and so learn words that reflect themselves.

Home word learning should be fun too. It is a time for all family members to get involved, enjoy words and learn something along the way. The energy of the school word learning environment should extend to home as well. By working together schools and families can have a greater impact on word learning than either can on their own.

Words are learnt as part of a whole language system and so for deep understanding it is crucial that new vocabulary is learnt in a child's home language as well. This can create some issues for home–school liaison, but the learning outcomes make it worthwhile.

References

Beck, I., McKeown, M. & Kucan, L. (2002). *Bringing Words to Life: Robust Vocabulary Instruction.* New York: Guilford Press.

Biemiller, A. (2005). Size and sequence in vocabulary development: Implications for choosing words for primary grade vocabulary instruction. In A. Hiebert & M. Kamil (Eds.), *Teaching and Learning Vocabulary: Bringing Research to Practice* (pp. 223–242). Mahwah, NJ: Lawrence Erlbaum Associates.

Block, C. C. & Mangieri, J. (2006). *The Vocabulary Enriched Classroom.* New York: Scholastic.

Chiat, S. (2000). *Understanding Children with Language Problems.* Cambridge: Cambridge University Press.

Clark, E. (1993). *The Lexicon in Acquisition.* Cambridge: Cambridge University Press.

Elleman, A., Endia, L., Morphy, P. & Compton, D. (2009). The impact of vocabulary instruction on passage-level comprehension of school-age children: A meta-analysis. *Journal of Research on Educational Effectiveness,* 21, 1–44.

Ford-Connors, E. & Paratore, J. (2015). Vocabulary instruction in fifth grade and beyond: Sources of word learning and productive contexts for development. *Review of Educational Research,* 85:1, 50–91.

Graves, M. F. (2015). Building a vocabulary program that really could make a significant contribution to students becoming college and career ready. In P.D. Pearson & E.H. Hiebert (Eds.), *Research-based Practices for Common Core Literacy* (pp. 123–142). New York: Teachers College Press.

Hayes, D. & Ahrens, M. (1988). Vocabulary simplification for children: A special case of "motherese"? *Journal of Child Language,* 15, 395–410.

Hart, B. & Risley, T. (1995). *Meaningful Differences in the Everyday Experience of Young American Children.* Baltimore, MD: Paul H. Brookes Publishing.

Hjetland, H., Brinchmann, E., Scherer, R. & Melby-Lervåg, M. (2017). *Preschool Predictors of Later Reading Comprehension Ability: A Systematic Review.* Oslo: Campbell Collaboration.

Law, J., Rush, R., Schoon, I. & Parsons, S. (2009). Modeling developmental language difficulties from school entry into adulthood: Literacy, mental health, and employment outcomes. *Journal of Speech, Language, and Hearing Research,* 52:6, 1401–1416.

Nash, H. & Snowling, M. (2006). Teaching new words to children with poor existing vocabulary knowledge: A controlled evaluation of the definition and context methods. *International Journal of Language & Communication Disorders,* 41:3, 335–354.

Nation, P. (1990). *Teaching and Learning Vocabulary.* New York: Newbury House.

Nelson, J. & Stage, S. (2007). Fostering the development of vocabulary knowledge and reading comprehension though contextually-based multiple meaning vocabulary instruction. *Education & Treatment of Children,* 30:1, 1–22.

Nippold, M.A. & Sun, L. (2008). Knowledge of morphologically complex words: A developmental study of older children and young adolescents. *Language, Speech and Hearing Services in Schools,* 39, 365–373.

Oakhill, J., Cain, K. & Elbro, C. (2014). *Understanding and Teaching Reading Comprehension: A Handbook.* London: Routledge.

Quigley, A. (2018). *Closing the Vocabulary Gap.* Abingdon, Oxon: Routledge.

Riccomini, P., Smith, G., Hughes, E. & Fries, K. (2015). The language of mathematics: The importance of teaching and learning mathematical vocabulary. *Reading & Writing Quarterly*, 31:3, 235–252.

Rice, M., Buhr, J. & Nemeth, M. (1990). Fast mapping word-learning abilities of language delayed pre-schoolers. *Journal of Speech and Hearing Research*, 55, 33–42.

Robson, S. (2006). *Developing Thinking and Understanding in Young Children: An Introduction for Students.* Abingdon, Oxon: Routledge.

Scott, J. & Nagy, W. (2004). Developing word consciousness. In J. F. Bauman & E. J. Kame'enui (Eds.), *Vocabulary Instruction: Research into Practice.* New York: Guilford Press.

Sparks, E. & Deacon, S. H. (2015). Morphological awareness and vocabulary acquisition: A longitudinal examination of their relationship in English-speaking children. *Applied Psycholinguistics*, 36, 299–321.

Spencer, M., Wagner, R. K. & Petscher, Y. (2019). The reading comprehension and vocabulary knowledge of children with poor reading comprehension despite adequate decoding: Evidence from a regression-based matching approach. *Journal of Educational Psychology*, 111, 1–14.

Spencer, S., Clegg, J., Stackhouse, J. & Rush, R. (2017). Contribution of spoken language and socio-economic background to adolescents' educational achievement at age 16 years. *International Journal of Language & Communication Disorders*, 52, 184–196.

Stahl, S. & Nagy, W. (2005). *Teaching Word Meanings.* Mahwah, NJ: Lawrence Erlbaum Associates.

Waldfogel, J. & Washbrook, E. (2010). *Low Income and Early Cognitive Development in the U.K.* London: Sutton Trust.

Wasik, B., Hindman, A. & Snell, E. (2016). Book reading and vocabulary development: A systematic review. *Early Childhood Research Quarterly*, 37, 39–57.

Wright, T. (2012). What classroom observations reveal about oral vocabulary instruction in kindergarten. *Reading Research Quarterly*, 47, 353–355.

Web references

Cain, K. & Oakhill, J. (2018). Vocabulary development and reading comprehension: A reciprocal relationship. In *Why Closing the Word Gap Matters*: *Oxford Language Report.* Oxford: Oxford University Press. https://oxford.ly/wordgap

Department for Education (2017). https://www.gov.uk/government/news/new-education-and-skills-measures-announced

Education Endowment Foundation (2019). *Oral Language Interventions* https://educationendow-mentfoundation.org.uk/evidence-summaries/teaching-learning-toolkit/oral-language-interventions/

National Curriculum (2014). *National Curriculum in England: Complete Framework for Key Sages 1 to 4 – For Teaching 1 September 2014 to 31 August 2015* https://www.gov.uk/government/publications/national-curriculum-in-england-framework-for-key-stages-1-to-4

Ofsted (2019). School Inspection Update January 2019 Special edition www.gov.uk/government/organisations/ofsted

Oxford University Press (2018). *Why Closing the Word Gap Matters: Oxford Language Report* https://oxford.ly/wordgap

Wegener, S. & Castles, A. (2018). How does oral vocabulary knowledge help children learn to read? https://www.teachermagazine.com.au/articles/how-does-oral-vocabulary-knowledge-help-children-learn-to-read?utm_source=CM&utm_medium=trending&utm_content=literacy

Implementing *Word Aware*

Word Aware: Quick Summary

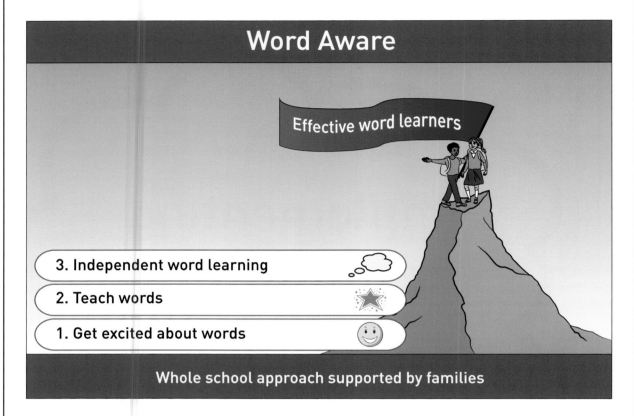

Vocabulary impacts on literacy skills, but also right across the curriculum and on life outcomes. It really is important, but because there are so many words to learn it cannot be fixed by a short-term intervention. Whole school communities need to work together.

Word Aware is built upon these three steps

1. Get excited about words: engage children with lots of interesting words at the right level. Play word games and enjoy vocabulary.

2. Teach words: explicit teaching of useful words. Only a small number can be taught, so they need to really count.

3. Independent word learning skills: children learn most words independently as they read and talk to others but teaching them how to do this will give word learning a boost.

Words are learnt in school and at home, so engaging families is fundamental to success.

In order to make a difference, vocabulary needs daily attention over long time periods from all of these angles.

Implementing *Word Aware*

Word Aware is a framework rather than an 'off the shelf intervention', and as such it needs to be applied to individual school contexts. The core principles and structures will remain the same, but what it looks like in practice may vary. And as a whole school approach implementing *Word Aware* requires whole school change.

In our experience, once teachers get onboard with *Word Aware* activities, they quickly become part of daily practice. However, to get going and to become consistent, requires planning, time, support and leadership. Implementing *Word Aware* will have much in common with other change processes but some points to consider include:

- Make sure all staff understand why *Word Aware* is being implemented, and understand the approach
- Work together to take a snapshot of current practice across the school, plan where you want to get to and how you will implement change
- Cultivate children and adults' love of words to drive the change process
- Develop consistency and quality before scaling up: start with small actions. Ensure the changes are embedded before moving on
- Set reasonable expectations for all and monitor how these are delivered
- Allow creativity where possible, and share ideas to inspire others
- Ensure that families are involved, and especially those of more vulnerable learners
- Measure outcomes and reflect on where you have come from. Celebrate success as well as make plans to improve
- Make a plan for maintaining the approach, particularly as staff leave or when attention moves to other initiatives.

Three Steps to Implementing Word Aware

The *Word Aware* approach to developing vocabulary is divided into three simple steps:

1. Get excited about words

2. Teach words: from content areas of the curriculum and from shared books

3. Independent word learning

These are the building blocks for effective vocabulary learning and work together as a cohesive unit. Once successfully implemented, the aim is that all children are motivated by words, they have a strong understanding of the most important words and they have the skills required to carry them forward on their word learning journey. By working together as a school and with families the aim is that all children will become effective word learners.

Start at the bottom of the 'mountain' by 'getting excited about words', then add 'teach words' and finally incorporate 'independent word learning'. The rationale of starting with 'Get excited about words' is that this will build energy and motivation as well as raise children's awareness of words. 'Teach words' is second in the process because it requires the most change, but also provides teachers and students with a great sense of progress. 'Teach words' is subdivided into words from the curriculum (STAR Topic) and from shared books (STAR Literacy). STAR Topic and STAR Literacy are different applications of the

same (Select-Teach-Activate-Review) process based on work by Blachowicz and Fisher (2015). It is recommended that STAR Topic goes first as this will allow practitioners to plan ahead and feel confident with the teaching process before the more spontaneous application used in STAR literacy. 'Independent word learning' is the final step because it requires a higher level of awareness of words and an ability to reflect on word learning, which are skills which have been developed in the previous steps. All three steps are continued, and overtime integrate into one cohesive multi-faceted approach.

Where to Start with *Word Aware*

Each part is summarised in the following 'where to start' guides. These are also provided within the individual sections. The guides provide a simple overview and a few ideas to get started. To fully implement the approach greater knowledge is required and this is provided in each part. The approach will also need to be applied to each school and class in different ways, so spend some time learning about *Word Aware*, reflecting on existing practice and building your plans.

Step 1

 1. Get Excited About Words

Promote staff interest in words.
Look at the staff activities (from page 30) and have fun with words.

Reflect on what activities you are already doing that get children excited about words. Think about both whole school as well as class-based activities. Then look at how you can make it even better. Start with easy to implement activities that will have a maximum impact in your school.

Celebrate words

- Choose a couple of activities to get adults excited by words. This could be word facts or jokes.

- Choose a couple of whole school activities from the examples provided on page 34. This could be 'whose favourite word?' (children match a word to a teacher, page 34), children writing their favourite word in chalk in the playground (page 35) or maybe a word challenge day (page 37).

- Every teacher chooses a couple of class-based activities from the examples starting on page 89. Each class may do something different. The activities should be easy to do, but really capture imagination. You could start with the 'Word Collector' bookmarks (page 92), create definition mobiles (page 117) or add gems to 'sparkling' vocabulary (page 99).

Play word games

- Choose four games that are new to you. Most of the games in this book are quick and require little preparation. Write them down somewhere to remind you. Teach them to any staff members who work with you in your classroom.

- Choose the best time to play games. This could be a game slot once a week, a quick game before you get down to work in the morning or to be used when concentration is waning. Establish the habit of playing games regularly.

Step 2

Two parts: STAR Topic and STAR Literacy both based on the same Select-Teach-Activate-Review process (Blachowicz & Fisher, 2015).

	2.1 Teach Words **STAR Topic**
Select	From one current maths/science/geography topic pick one 'Goldilocks' word: a word that is really useful and will be encountered again.
Teach	Teach the word quickly using the STAR Topic Word Wizard. Once confident, aim for this process to take five minutes. 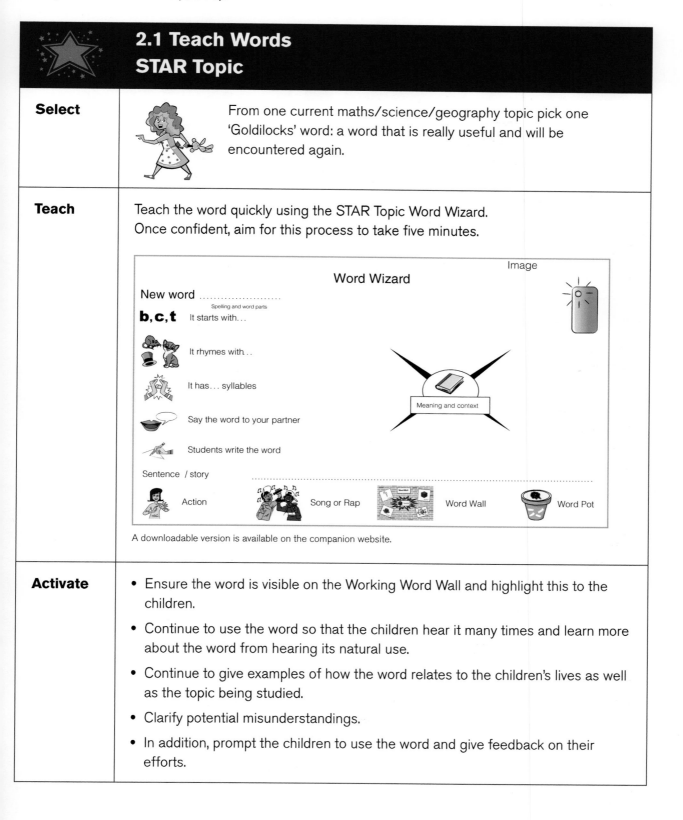 A downloadable version is available on the companion website.
Activate	• Ensure the word is visible on the Working Word Wall and highlight this to the children. • Continue to use the word so that the children hear it many times and learn more about the word from hearing its natural use. • Continue to give examples of how the word relates to the children's lives as well as the topic being studied. • Clarify potential misunderstandings. • In addition, prompt the children to use the word and give feedback on their efforts.

Review	• Review the word at the end of the lesson
	• Play a Word Wall clue game once a week, e.g. Fly swat game (see page 183)
	• Take ten words out of the Word Pot each week and talk about them (see page 169). This could be two words every day or five words twice a week.
	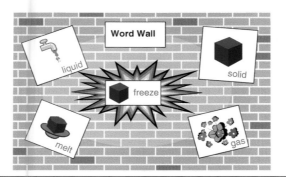 

When **starting** to use *Word Aware* begin with teaching **two words a week**. These could be either STAR Topic words or STAR Literacy or one of each. Once confident with the process then build up to teaching a word a day (**five words a week**).

2.2 Teach Words
STAR Literacy

| **Select** | | From your current whole class book pick a Goldilocks word: a word that is really useful and will be encountered again. |

| **Teach** | Teach the word via either the Word Wizard, page 172 (if you want to write the information down) or the 'A new word in nine steps', page 222 (if you would prefer to do it verbally). Once confident, aim for either of these processes to take five minutes. |
| | 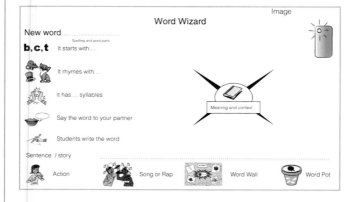  |

Activate		**Choose a few relevant questions to activate the students' understanding of the word. These questions work for any part of speech.**
	General	Which one of these is right? E.g. Who would **waddle**, a duck or a lion?
		Describe the word to your friend.
	Reflection	Finish this: I like/don't like this word because …
		What do you learn by knowing this word?
		How does the word make you feel?
	Contexts	Where might you see this word?
		Think of a time when you could use this word
		Finish this: In the book it was used like this…, but it can be used like this too…
		Given a context and the word, what would else would you observe? e.g.: If the house was **dilapidated**, what would you see?
		Think of two uses for this word to show how the word can be used differently.
		Act out a situation which shows the meaning of the word.
	Synonyms	Think of another word that might mean something similar to this word.
		This word is a bit like … How is it different from that word?
		What's the first word that jumps into your head when you hear the word?
		The author chose this word. What other word could they have used?
	Linking	Think of three words linked to the new word.
		If this word was a (car/animal/food) what would it be? Why?

<table>
<tr>
<td rowspan="2">**Review**</td>
<td>
- Review the word at the end of the lesson
- Play a Word Wall clue game once a week, e.g. Fly swat game (see page 183)
- Take ten words out of the Word Pot each week and talk about them (see page 169).
</td>
</tr>
<tr>
<td>
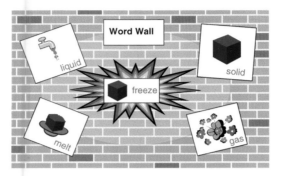 
</td>
</tr>
</table>

When **starting** to use *Word Aware* begin with teaching **two words a week**. These could be either STAR Topic words or STAR Literacy or one of each. Once confident with the process then build up to teaching a word a day (**five words a week**).

Step 3

3. Independent Word Learning

- Make a judgement about your class's word learning skills using the checklists on page 247 for children under 7 and the one on page 249 if they are over 7.
- Choose one area to focus on. Choose a strategy that you ticked as 'some' children are already using.
- Teach strategies to the whole class.
- Embed strategies into day-to-day conversations.
- Move on to the next skill and repeat.

Implementing *Word Aware* Over a School Year (and Beyond)

Successful implementation of *Word Aware* will take time and organisation. A suggested timeframe of implementation is given on the next page. This is just a guide and can be altered to fit in with your school. Go at a rate that works for you. This implementation plan could easily be stretched over a two-year period. Once the approach is fully embedded into your school, it is important that effective vocabulary teaching remains part of daily practice. Like any other element of teaching, vocabulary teaching needs on-going refresher training and monitoring. Throughout the vocabulary journey it is important to keep the sense of fun. Whenever you spend time as a staff team focusing on vocabulary, incorporate some sort of word game. A selection of adult activities is given starting on page 30.

References

Blachowicz, C. & Fisher, P. (2015). *Teaching Vocabulary in All Classrooms*, 5th edition. New York: Pearson.

Implementing Word Aware Over a School Year

 Term 1 (6 weeks)

Introduce basic principles of *Word Aware*. Audit current practice.

Get excited: get everyone (including teachers) excited about words. Whole school events, class activities, games, engage parents. Monitor regularity of activities to ensure consistency.

 Term 2 (6 weeks)

Get excited: continue to celebrate words and play word games on a weekly basis. Continue to monitor frequency.

Teach words: start to teach two words a week in each class. These may be topic-based words, words from whole class books or one of each. Monitor consistency of implementations, particularly support consistency of reviewing words.

Families: run events to get families involved, informed and excited.

 Term 3 (6 weeks)

Get excited: continue to celebrate words and play word games on a weekly basis. Continue to monitor frequency.

Teach words: keep teaching two words a week. By the end of this six weeks (i.e. been regularly teaching two words a week for 12 weeks) word teaching is now consistent (including reviewing words) and embedded in planning and the actual teaching of words should take no more than five minutes.

 Term 4 (6 weeks)

Get excited: continue to celebrate words and play word games on a weekly basis. Continue to monitor frequency.

Teach words: continue to teach two words a week.

Develop independent skills: identify gaps in skills. Target gaps within literacy (language arts) or other lessons. Have focused activities once per week.

 & **Term 5 & 6 (12 weeks) and beyond**

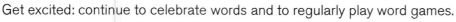

Get excited: continue to celebrate words and to regularly play word games.

Teach words: once two words are consistently taught each week, they are taught quickly (five minutes) and they are then consistently activated and reviewed then the number of words can be gradually increased. The aim is to build up to five words a week.

Develop independent strategies: develop whole school processes for teaching word learning strategies integrated within the curriculum.

Ensure consistency, make sure all word learning is embedded into planning and don't forget to have fun.

Get Excited About Words

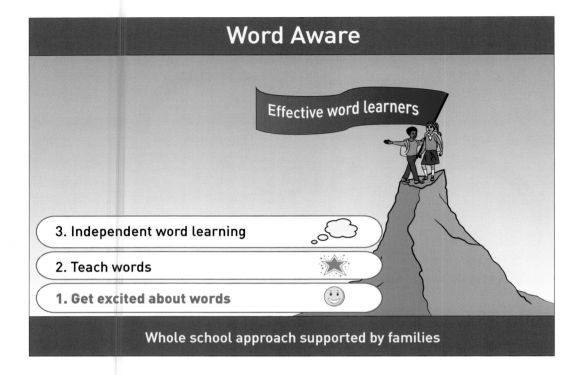

The word learning environment is crucial as it forms the foundation upon which any successful vocabulary intervention is built. Children are born word learners and they will develop vocabulary naturally through exposure (Chiat, 2000). However, by enriching the word learning environment and exposing children to a wider range of words, practitioners are able to give students more opportunities to expand their vocabularies (Scott & Nagy, 2009). As you develop the language environment be careful to make it appropriately challenging. There is a potential to bombard children with language, and this may be counterproductive.

It has been estimated that each child needs to learn seven words per day throughout their schooling if they are to reach the average of knowing 30,000 words by adulthood (Clark, 1993). It is not practical or possible to reach this target via direct teaching alone. Direct teaching has a part to play, and this is expanded in later parts, but enriching the word learning environment remains crucial.

Enriching the word learning environment is not about one major change, but rather about creating a culture in which practitioners are able to reflect and make small changes that suit the children in their classes. Most classrooms will have much in place already, and so the first step in creating an enriched word learning environment is to reflect upon current practice.

It may be tempting to think that the word-enriched environment is mere 'background' that can be skipped over in the rush to get to the direct teaching elements. However, small changes in daily practice will greatly increase children's opportunities for word learning. A word-enriched environment will provide opportunities to learn words independently as well as reinforce words that have been taught via other elements of the *Word Aware* approach. We have chosen it as the starting point for implementing *Word Aware*, because it creates a buzz and energy around word learning which can then be built upon.

Two parts to get excited about words:

- Celebrate words: activities and actions which promote enjoyment of the spoken and written word
- Play word games: fun activities that encourage word play, which promotes enjoyment of words, but also allows for new connections to be made. Word learning without knowing about it!

Come together as a school and reflect on what you are doing already to promote children's enjoyment of words. Get creative and bounce ideas off each other, add in the ideas contained in this book and make a plan to get children truly excited about words. In your plan build in whole school events and opportunities for families to get involved so that the whole school community becomes abuzz with words. The mere mention of 'words' can instil fear in some children and adults, so make your activities inclusive so that everyone can participate and benefit.

 ## 1. Get Excited About Words: Where to Start

Get <u>staff</u> excited about words. Look at the staff activities (see page 30) and try a few or add your own ideas.

Reflect on what activities you are already doing that get children excited about words. Think about both whole school as well as class-based activities. Then look at how you can make it even better. Start with easy to implement activities that will have maximum impact across the school.

Celebrate words

- Choose a couple of whole school activities from the examples provided on page 34. You could start with 'whose favourite word?' (children match a word to a teacher, page 34), children writing their favourite word in chalk in the playground (page 35) or maybe a word challenge day (page 37).
- Every class chooses a couple of class-based activities from the examples on page 89. Each class can do something different. It should be something that is easy to do that really captures your class's imagination. You could start with the 'Word Collector' bookmarks (page 92), create definition mobiles (page 117) or add gems to 'sparkling' vocabulary (page 99).

Play word games

- Choose four or so games that are new to you. Most of the games in this book are quick and require little preparation. Write them down somewhere to remind you. Teach them to any staff members who work with you in your classroom.
- Choose the best time to play games. This could be a game slot once a week, a quick game before you get down to work in the morning or to be used when concentration is waning. Establish the habit of playing games regularly.

The aim of these activities and games is to enthral and inspire and not overwhelm.

Once you have got started and built up some momentum it is easy to keep going. Add in more creative whole school activities and build up your repertoire of ways to celebrate words in your class. Keep trialling new words games and make up a class collection, so that students can then browse and play them on their own. Add in your own ideas and show your love of words.

1.1 Celebrate Words

Staff Activities

In order to get children excited by words, staff also need to be excited by them. Incorporate word play into staff meetings and activities for the staffroom. It may seem hard to justify spending time on a game when there is so much work to get through but if adults are to show true enjoyment of words, they need to have fun too. These activities are aimed at adults not children.

Staff notice board

Create a space on your staff noticeboard to add any interesting facts, competitions or jokes about words.

Favourite word

Spend time talking about your favourite words. This is a great activity to start with when introducing *Word Aware*.

Twitter

Follow vocabulary-related posts on Twitter. Start with @susie_dent and @WordAware.

Play word games

Play word games in staff meetings. Many of the games listed in this section are enjoyable for adults to play too. They may be used as a break in a business meeting or training session.

Crosswords

Have crosswords available in the staffroom. There are lots of crosswords available from newspapers as well as puzzle websites such as https://simplydailypuzzles.com/daily-quick-crossword/.

Book clubs, book recommendations, book sharing

Encourage staff to read for pleasure. That is the single best thing anyone can do to improve their own vocabulary.

Different languages

Do you have staff that speak different languages? Can they teach words to other staff? Try writing a word on the board. How many languages can the staff group translate it into? Compare pronunciation similarities and investigate etymology. Have fun looking at direct translation of proverbs and non-English words that are not translatable. Some examples can be found below.

Words we don't have in English

aldeinsamkeit	German	The feeling of solitude and connectedness to nature when being alone in the woods.
wabi-sabi	Japanese	Finding beauty in imperfections.
saudade	Portuguese	The feeling of longing for an absent something or someone that you love but which might never return.
ya'aburnee	Arabic	A declaration of one's hope to die before another person because of how unbearable it would be to live without them.
yuánfèn	Mandarin	The fate between two people.
forelsket	Norwegian	The euphoria experienced as you begin to fall in love.
kilig	Tagalog	The feeling of butterflies in your stomach, usually when something romantic takes place.
commuovere	Italian	A heart-warming story that moved you to tears.
hiraeth	Welsh	A particular type of longing for the homeland or the romanticised past.
mamihlapinatapei	Yagan	The wordless, meaningful look shared by two people who both desire to initiate something but are both reluctant to do so.
toska	Russian	A sensation of great spiritual anguish, often without a specific cause; a longing with nothing to long for.
depaysement	French	The feeling that comes from not being in one's home country; being a foreigner.
duende	Spanish	A work of art's mysterious power to deeply move a person.

https://www.ef.com/wwen/blog/language/13-words-with-no-english-translation/

Word jokes for adults

Sometimes they can be silly childish jokes, other times more complex word play jokes. Here are a few to get you going

Q: Why was six scared of seven? A: Because seven ate nine.
Q: Why couldn't the leopard play hide and seek? A: Because he was always spotted.
Man walks into a tavern . . . oh you won't get it, it's an Inn joke.
Did a gig at a conference for sufferers of extreme acne. Told my first joke, the place erupted.
Never leave sulphuric acid in a metal beaker. That's an oxidant waiting to happen.
Before he died my Dad used to drive a digger. At his funeral his colleagues said that now he's gone he's left behind a hole that will never be filled.
My credit card company sent me a camouflaged bull. It's the hidden charges you have to watch out for.
I've been trying to write puns about sword fighting but I couldn't think of any words with a dual meaning.
I used to have a job drilling holes for water. It was well boring.
Someone hit me with a sweet-smelling burning stick! I was incensed.
I'm not very tech savvy. Maybe it's my age. I've been trying to download this video on incontinence. Problem is, it's just continually streaming.

https://www.mirror.co.uk/news/weird-news/britains-best-word-play-uk-5148341

Word of the week

Send or post a word of the week (or word fact) aimed at staff. @susie_dent tweets an amazing array of entertaining words, word history and word-related trivia. This is not about teaching staff new words: the aim is to interest and entertain staff. Here are a few examples from Susie Dent's Twitter feed that could be shared with staff or added to noticeboards.

Interesting words and word facts for adults

Cacoethes [kak-o-ee-thees] is the desperate urge to do something very inadvisable.
Matutinal: chirpy and cheery first thing. Annoy other people with it and you're a 'gigglemug'.
Groaking is an old Scots word for the act of silently and enviously watching someone eat something delicious. Can be used of dogs, humans around chips, and anyone watching cooking on TV.
Quiddle: to spend time on trivial tasks as a way of avoiding the important ones.
Moodle: to busy oneself in an unmethodical and entirely ineffectual manner.
Boondoggle: to spend time on a project you'll ultimately regret.
Lalochezia: the release of stress and frustration through swearing.
Bloviator (19th century): a speaker of empty rhetoric and blower of hot air; someone who talks a lot but says very little.
A mumpsimus (16th century) is someone who refuses to budge/insists that they are right, despite clear evidence that they are wrong. Plural: mumpsimuses.
The word lucifugal [loose-if-few-gul] means 'fleeing the light', e.g. peeking out from the duvet and promptly diving back under.
Respair, a word from centuries ago, is the recovery from despair. To respair is to have fresh hope.
If you're a lover/addict of tea then, according to the dictionary (and the poet Shelley), you're a theist.
Ipsedixitism is the dogmatic assertion that something is true because someone, somewhere said it, and without offering any supporting evidence whatsoever. (From the Latin for 'he said it').

From @susie_dent

Whole School Events

Whole school events that target vocabulary will give words and word learning a profile in your school. They will engage parents, but also act as a motivator for children. Here are some ideas to get you started.

Whose favourite word?

Ask all the teachers what their favourite word is. Write each one on a separate piece of paper. Stick these on (ground floor) classroom windows which face the playground. Challenge children to match the words with the corresponding staff member. A great way for getting the children talking about words. Thanks to Kingsgate Primary School, London, for this idea.

The Word Collector

Read *The Word Collector* (Reynolds, 2018) in assembly. This presents as a book for younger children but in fact works well across the primary range. The story describes how a boy goes through life collecting and then sharing words. This book is a great introduction to independent word learning skills as outlined in step 3.

Tree of words

Cut out a large tree trunk and branches and display on a wall in a public area. Children and family members then write down their favourite word on coloured leaves and attach them to the tree. The tree comes to life as more leaves are added. Words may be written in any language.

Video interview

The children interview peers, teachers, parents or visitors to the school about their favourite words. Videos can then be shown on school websites, in reception areas or in assemblies.

Invited authors and poets

When authors and poets are invited into school, ask them questions about words. What is their favourite word? What do they think of words? How do they make words fun?

Word Clouds

Each child is asked to name their favourite word and these are made into a word cloud using free websites such as wordle.com, wordclouds.com, wordart.com or tagcrowd.com. The resultant images can then be displayed together or outside each class. Staff and families may also contribute and potentially a whole school word cloud could be created.

Chalked up

Using chalk children write words that they like on the playground asphalt. Photographs may be taken as a record. Children should be encouraged to ask each other about why they like the words they have chosen and about their meaning and use.

Family word workshop

This can be for all families or for groups of invited parents. The purpose of these workshops is to involve families in vocabulary learning. From our experience, sessions work best if there is a combination of hands-on activities with families and a little bit of knowledge sharing. Activities could include:

- Key messages about word learning, including how they can work jointly with the school.

- Vocabulary-related activities and events, such as 'Word of the Week' (p 39) that will be happening and how they can get involved.

- An outline of how vocabulary is being taught in school and the homework tasks such as Fridge Words (p 209) which will be sent home.

- Making things that children can use in school such as 'vocabulators' (p 200), fortune tellers (p 201), magic books (p 202) or folding true or false books (p 198).

- Children teaching their parents word games that they have been playing in school. Ideally these are games with few or no resources.

- Admiring children's creations, such as favourite word costumes, art or craft work with related vocabulary or stories with sparkling vocabulary.

- Contributing their favourite word to a whole school 'tree of words' or word cloud.

Further details for involving families are provided from page 313.

Vocabulary assemblies

Holding vocabulary assemblies where each class nominates a word they discovered in their class book and prizes are given for the most interesting word. A 'word cup' can be given out each week, with the word going in the school's newsletter or added to a specific display. A variation is to have a soft toy as the weekly award. Alliterative names work well, so dependent on the animal you could have a 'Word Wombat, Word Walrus or Word Whale.'

Whole school competitions

Run whole school competitions focused on vocabulary. These can be overseen by a 'Word Aware panel' of students who choose and advertise the competitions as well as select the winners. Suggestions for word games are outlined below. Add your own ideas also, but make sure the games are about engaging children's interest in words and focus on word meaning.

- Three words to describe: each child draws a self-portrait and adds three positive words which describe themselves.
- Each child illustrates a word that they found during reading or have learnt recently.
- Verb videos: children/small groups make short videos of themselves acting out verbs.
- Adjective photo: each child chooses an adjective and then takes a photo that exemplifies the adjective.
- Poems/short stories: children are challenged to write a poem or short story containing or titled with, a given word. Different words may be selected for each year group.
- Word friends: children are encouraged to listen out to words that their friends say. When they hear a great word, they record it and enter it in a competition. The prize is given to the child who used the word and the nominee. A form to fill in could be something along the lines of 'My friend. . . . used a great word when he/she was talking about. . . . He/she said. . . . I think this word is particularly great because . . .'
- Make up words that fill the gaps where no words exist. For instance, what word would you use to describe that weird face people make as they reach to finish a videocall? Or try combining words to make new ones, such as when 'chill' and 'relax' got combined to form 'chillax'.
- Children select any word and show its meaning in the shape of the word. 'Mournful' could be in the shape of a sad mouth. 'Haphazard' would be written in a random style.
- Words around the school: ten to 20 words are selected that have some connection with different areas of the school. These are displayed around the school, but their link to the area they are displayed in is kept secret. The challenge is to find the words and then work out how they are linked to that location. Below are example words, their location and an explanation of how the word may be linked to that location.

Word	Location	Link
Cacophony	Dining hall	The sound of the voices echoing around the dining hall.
Orderly	Lining up location	Students are expected to line up in an orderly fashion.
Saunter	Corridor	Some students saunter along the corridor instead of walking quickly.
Historic	Reception area	There are photographs and objects on display which show the school's history.
Scavenge	Outdoor bin	When the playground is empty, birds come and scavenge food from the bin.
Triumphant	Basketball goal	The team who scores the most goals is triumphant.
Bellow	Stage	The actors bellow from the stage to make themselves heard.

Word	Location	Link
Vibrant	Display board	The artwork on display has used a vibrant array of colours.
Mayhem	Playground	With so many children playing at break times it can look like mayhem.
Famished	Kitchen	Before lunch children may feel famished.
Secretive	Staff room	Children do not know what conversations teachers have in the staff room.

Word Aware days

Dressing up as a favourite word.

There is lots of information on setting up vocabulary parades on the link below, including a slide show of example costumes to inspire you: https://www.debrafrasier.com/vocabulary-parades/

Many schools have held creative alternatives which still effectively celebrate words but make less organisational demands. Alternatives include hat parades, decorating paper tabards in school and dressing up in any costume and thinking of the word once in school.

Dressing up as your favourite word is a great way to get the whole school community excited about words. Use this opportunity to involve families. Invite families into school to watch a parade. Once they are in school, combine this with playing some word games with their children and learning about why vocabulary is so important. See page 313 onwards 'Families' for further details.

As part of 'No pens day Wednesday'

'No pens day Wednesday' was originally developed by the Communication Trust. For one day. children and adults are not permitted to write (with a pen or on a computer) and so the focus is on spoken language. This break from routine is challenging, but it brings about a natural focus on language. For more information go to https://ican.org.uk/no-pens-day-wednesday/. This is usually in October/ November. The website contains a wealth of useful resources.

Word Challenge day

All children are sent home with a word challenge on the same day. The challenge will vary according to the age of the children. Suggested activities include:

- Use a specific word in context at home that evening or when talking on the way home. Can other family members spot the challenging word, or was it used seamlessly?

- Find an interesting word in a different language. Bring back the word to school with a translation. Use the book *Lost in Translation: An Illustrated Compendium of Untranslatable Words from Around the World* by Ella Frances Sanders (2014), as an inspiration.

- Send a list of words home for children to ask their families to define. Use the sheet on page 303. For multilingual families, their job is to translate English words into their home language (see page 304). Words sent home could be from a topic you are about to teach, from a book/ chapter the class is about to read, words related to a place you are going to visit or words related to school values.

- Send home the 'My treasure chest words' sheet on page 94. The challenge is for children to fill out the sheet with three words that they like from the book they are reading, words used on TV, online or used at home in conversation.

- Each child identifies a word from their 'Word Collector' bookmark (page 92) to find out about.

- 'Word Expert': each child is sent home with a new word to ask family members about. Encourage families to look up and learn about the word together.

- Send home 'Finding different words' bookmarks (page 93) and encourage all children to talk about words with their parents when they read that night.

Word bunting

On both sides of a triangular piece of card write and illustrate a new word. The paper is then attached to a string and used to decorate the classroom or corridor. Thank you to St Ninian's Primary School for this idea.

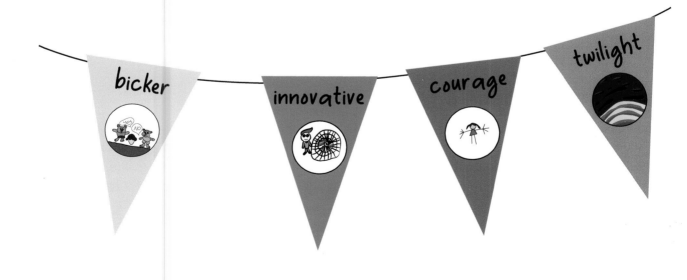

Word of the week

Each week an interesting word is displayed where children and families can see it. Along with each word there is a simple meaning and a task that children can engage with, both at home and at school. The definitions are deliberately simple without reference to multiple meanings. It is important that both school and home celebrate children's responses. There are ninety or so words here for each age group which allows for one word a week for thirty weeks of the year, and so is enough to cover a child's primary/elementary schooling. To allow for flexible usage the words, the meanings and challenges are provided in the following formats:

1. Posters for display. Examples on pages 40 and 41.

2. A smaller version that can be cut and pasted onto websites, newsletters etc.

3. Text only versions that can be sent via text messages.

All three resources are available to download from the companion website which accompanies this book.

There is also an additional poster for children whose home language is not English (see Home Language Challenge poster on page 42). The challenge is for the family to translate the word into their home language and talk about it. **Any vocabulary homework should be completed in a child's home language. Learning a word in one language will support English language learning.**

> Note: This is a 'get excited about words' activity, not a teaching activity
>
> The aim of this activity is to raise the profile of words and to have fun. This activity only gives a simple meaning and one challenge. This is not enough to learn a word in depth. If you want to go further and effectively teach these words you will need to use the process as outlined in Step 2.2: Teach words: STAR Literacy, see page 212.

Examples of Word of the Week poster

The first one is aimed at children under 7, the second over 7.

Word of the Week

discover

Meaning

When you find something you did not know before

Challenge

Imagine you find an old box in a cupboard. What do you think you could **discover** inside?

CELEBRATING WORDS

Word of the Week

fascinated

Meaning	**Challenge**
You are really interested in something and you keep thinking about it	What things are you *fascinated* by?

CELEBRATING WORDS

Home Language Challenge poster

NEW WORDS

sabada	okwu
kelimeler	parole
mots	besede
slowa	woorden
slova	shabdon

Can you speak another language?

Challenge:
Your challenge is to find out what this word is in your home language.

Look the words up with someone in your family.

_____

C E L E B R A T I N G   W O R D S

The definitions are based on Collins Cobuild Primary Learner's Dictionary (2018) and the Collins online dictionary.

Words for younger children

Word	Definition	Challenge
ancient	Really old.	If a building was **ancient**, what would it look like?
anxiously	Being worried as you do something.	Imagine you are **anxiously** waiting for something to happen. You are worried about it. What might you be **anxious** about?
astonished	Really surprised.	What could you do tonight that would make family members **astonished**?
bellow	To shout with an angry, loud, deep voice.	Think of another word that is a bit like **bellowed**. Do others at home agree with you? Can they think of other words that have similar meanings?

Word	Definition	Challenge
blend	To mix something together so it makes one thing.	Listen and look out for the word. Where might you see it or hear it?
boom	A loud, deep sound.	Do you know anyone that has a **booming** voice? Say your name in a **booming** voice.
captive	Not being able to get away.	How does the word **captive** make you feel? Why?
cautiously	Carefully because you don't want something to go wrong.	What might you do **cautiously**? Would you be **cautious** crossing a road, when on a high climbing frame or trying food you don't know?
clench	Holding tightly because you are angry.	**Clench** your fists and your jaw and make a face to go with how you might be feeling.

Word	Definition	Challenge
cling	To hold very tightly.	What things might you **cling** to? Why?
clogged	When something is blocked up.	This one is disgusting! At home find out what happens when drains get **clogged**.
courageous	Brave or not afraid.	When have you done something that was **courageous**? Something that is very brave.
creep	To move somewhere quietly and slowly.	Act out **creep**. Can others at home guess the word you are acting out?
cunning	Clever and sometimes trying to cheat.	Can you think of a book character who is **cunning**?

Word	Definition	Challenge
curious	You are interested and want to know more.	Act out **curious**, showing how you feel with your face and body language.
damp	A bit wet.	Imagine your clothes are **damp**. How do they feel?
departed	Leave somewhere.	Where might you see the word **depart** a lot?
determined	When someone is sure they want to do something, even if it is difficult.	Ask someone at home to say the word **determined** in a sentence.
discover	When you find something that you did not know before.	Imagine you found an old box in a cupboard. What do you think you could **discover** inside?

Word	Definition	Challenge
disguise	You try and look different, so people do not recognise you.	What **disguise** would you like?
draught	A stream of cold air that comes into a room.	Ask someone at home to find out what **draught** means by looking up the word on their phone and tell you what it means.
dread	Worried about something because you think it will be bad.	Everyone dreads something. Ask people at home what they might **dread**.
drifting	To float along in water or in air.	How does the word **drifting** make you feel? Why?
drizzling	Light rain.	If it was **drizzling** today, would you like to be inside or outside? When was the last time it was **drizzling**?

Word	Definition	Challenge
dull	A colour that is not very bright. Weather can also be dull: not very bright.	Ask someone at home to say the word **dull** in a sentence.
eager	Want to do something very much.	What is something you are **eager** about? What are others at home **eager** about?
echo	A sound that you hear again.	Imagine you are in a long tunnel. Can someone else pretend to be your **echo**?
eerie	Strange and frightening.	What places might be **eerie**?
elegant	Stylish, graceful.	Pretend you are really **elegant** as you walk.

Word	Definition	Challenge
emerge	To come out from a place.	Tell someone about dinosaurs or chicks coming out of eggs. Use the word **emerge**.
exclaimed	Speaking suddenly or loudly as you are excited, angry or shocked.	Listen and look out for the word. Where might you see it or hear it? Books often have this word.
expert	Someone who knows a lot about something.	What things are you **expert** about?
familiar	Something you know well.	Listen and look out for the word **familiar**. Where might you see it or hear it?
frustrated	To get upset because you can't sort out a problem.	Act out being **frustrated**, showing it with your face and body.

Word	Definition	Challenge
furious	Really angry.	Can you think of a time when someone was **furious**? What did they look or sound like? Act out being **furious**.
gasped	To quickly breathe in because you are surprised or shocked.	When have you **gasped**? What book characters might **gasp**?
gestures	What you do with your hands to help explain what you feel or want to say.	Spend the day watching the **gestures** other people use. How many different gestures can you see?
gloomy	So dark that you can't see very well.	How does the word **gloomy** make you feel? Why?
glorious	Something that is beautiful and amazing.	Find a **glorious** picture. Talk about it with someone and tell them why it is **glorious**.

Word	Definition	Challenge
gurgle	A noise a baby makes when they are happy or a noise water makes.	Ask someone at home to pretend to **gurgle** like a baby.
guzzle	To eat or drink quickly. You are being greedy!	When you see someone drinking quickly, think of the word **guzzle** (you don't need to tell them!)
hesitate	When someone waits for a little bit because they are worried what to do or say.	Watch out for when you see other people **hesitate**. How long are they waiting before they speak?
hollow	Objects with space inside.	Find three things at home that are **hollow**.
hopeful	Thinking something you want will probably happen.	Think of something that you are **hopeful** about. What are you hoping will happen?

Word	Definition	Challenge
howl	A long, loud crying sound.	What animals are good at **howling**?
hurl	To throw something. You use a lot of energy to throw it really hard.	Think of another word that is a bit like **hurled**. Do others at home agree with you? Can they think of other words that have similar meanings?
immense	Really big.	What things can you think of that are **immense**?
irresistible	Something is so good that you can't stop yourself doing or having it.	What things do you find **irresistible**?
magnificent	Something that is extremely good, beautiful, or impressive.	What things do you think are **magnificent**? What have you done that is **magnificent**?

Word	Definition	Challenge
miserable	Very unhappy.	What things make you **miserable**?
mysterious	Something that is strange that you don't know or understand.	Act out being **mysterious** and say the word in a **mysterious** way.
notice	To be aware of something.	Close your eyes and listen. What are the sounds you **notice**?
occasion	When an important thing happens.	Listen and look out for the word **occasion**. Where might you see it or hear it?
overhead	Something that is above you.	Imagine you are at the funfair. What might be **overhead**?

Word	Definition	Challenge
panicky	Feeling so worried or afraid that you can't think clearly.	What things make you **panicky**? What things make others **panicky**?
peer	To look hard because it is very hard to see.	When might you need to **peer**?
perhaps	You are not sure, but it might be true.	Count how many times people at home use the word **perhaps** in sentences. Set a family record!
rundown	Not looked after so it is a bit broken and doesn't work very well.	Spot things on your way home that look **rundown**.
scavenge	Animals or people do this when they are looking through lots of things nobody else wants.	Rats, seagulls, foxes, hyenas all **scavenge**. What do they like to **scavenge** for?

Word	Definition	Challenge
screech	A loud high noise. It isn't very nice!	If someone was **screeching**. How would it make you feel? Why?
scrumptious	Really tasty.	Think of five things that are **scrumptious**.
secretive	Trying to hide something from other people.	What might you be **secretive** about? What wouldn't you want other people to know?
shaky	Your body is wobbly because you are scared or ill.	Can you pretend to be so scared that you are **shaky**?
shriek	To give a short, very loud cry.	Who at home **shrieks** the most? When do they **shriek**?

Word	Definition	Challenge
shudder	You shook because you were cold, frightened or disgusted.	Pretend you are feeling scared. It makes you **shudder**.
sly	Someone who tries to hide what they want or feel. They are good at tricking people.	When might it be a good time to be **sly**?
smothered	Cover something over.	Who in your family **smothers** their toast with jam?
sneak	To go somewhere very quietly.	Try and **sneak** in somewhere without anyone noticing.
spectacular	Amazing, big, dramatic.	What things can you think of that are **spectacular**?

Word	Definition	Challenge
splendid	Very good.	How does the word **splendid** make you feel? Why?
spluttered	Making short sounds when talking, because you are upset or embarrassed.	Act out **spluttering**. Can others guess the word you are acting out?
squeal	A long, squeaky sound.	What animals might **squeal**? Draw one.
stagger	When you can't walk straight because you are ill or drunk.	Pretend to **stagger**. Who at home can **stagger** the best?
steady	Not moving or shaking.	Who in your house has the steadiest hand? Build a tall tower of bricks to prove it or play Jenga.

Word	Definition	Challenge
stern	Very serious and a little bit cross.	Who sometimes looks a bit **stern**? Make a **stern** face.
stiff	Something that does not bend easily.	Pretend you are **stiff** and can't bend. How will you walk?
stroll	Walking slowly in a relaxed way.	Act out **stroll**. Can others guess?
stuffy	A room that is too hot and there isn't enough air.	Ask someone at home to say the word **stuffy** in a sentence.

Word	Definition	Challenge
surrounded	All around.	When would it be good to be **surrounded**? When would it be bad to be **surrounded**?
swoop	A bird suddenly flies downward.	Pretend to **swoop**. Which animals might **swoop**?
terrified	Really scared.	Some people are **terrified** of spiders, snakes, high places or dogs. How do you feel when you are **terrified**? How do you show it?
thundering	A loud, deep noise. Can be about the weather.	How does the word **thundering** make you feel?

Word	Definition	Challenge
tremendous	Very good, amazing.	How many times could you find to use the word **tremendous**? Tell someone that their writing, drawing or acting is **tremendous** when they do it really well.
tug	A quick, strong pull.	Why shouldn't you **tug** a dog's tail? How does it feel if someone **tugs** your hair?
twinkling	A light that keeps getting brighter and then less bright.	Think of two objects that you can describe as **twinkling**.
vanish	To go away suddenly.	Magicians make things **vanish**. They seem to go away. If you were a magician what would you make **vanish**?
vast	Really big.	If you had a **vast** house, how many rooms would it have? Imagine walking through the **vast** house.

Word	Definition	Challenge
wail	A long, loud sound you make because you are sad or hurt.	Ask family members if they can remember a time when you **wailed**? What happened to make you **wail**?
wheeze	If someone wheezes, they find it hard breathing and make a whistling sound.	Pretend to **wheeze**. Do you know anyone who **wheezes** (without pretending)?

Words for older children

Word	Definition	Challenge
aloof	Someone who is not very friendly and does not like spending time with other people	Sometimes people are **aloof** and sometimes they are **shy**. What's the difference?
anticipation	Feeling excited about something that is going to happen.	When is the last time you felt **anticipation**? Describe how it felt in your body.
ashamed	To feel embarrassed or guilty because of something you have done.	If someone is feeling **ashamed**, what might have they done?
banish	If someone or something is **banished** it is sent away and stopped from coming back.	If you were **banished** to your room what might you have done? If someone was **banished** from a club, what could have happened?
beckoned	To use your hand to ask someone to come to you.	Show how you can **beckon** someone to come to you. When do you need to **beckon**?

Word	Definition	Challenge
berserk	Crazy and out of control.	Slip **berserk** into conversation with a classmate or family member and see if they notice.
bustling	Moving in a hurried way, often because they are very busy.	What places do you know that are **bustling**? Are different times of the day **bustling**?
cantankerous	Someone who is always finding things to argue and complain about.	Look **cantankerous** up in a thesaurus. Find a synonym that you know well and ask someone from your family about how the two words are the same and different.
cascade	Lots of water flowing downwards, very quickly.	How does the word **cascade** make you feel?
clutching	To hold something really tightly because you are afraid or worried.	What and why would you want to **clutch** onto something?

Word	Definition	Challenge
colossal	Really big.	What things could you call **colossal**?
content	Fairly happy. Satisfied.	When is it good to feel **content** and when is it not so good? Discuss this with your family. You might have different views!
cosmopolitan	A cosmopolitan place or society is full of people from many different cultures.	How **cosmopolitan** is your school? Which places can be described as **cosmopolitan**?
crestfallen	You are sad and disappointed about something.	If you were feeling **crest-fallen**, what might have just happened?
curiously	In an interesting way.	Think of fictional characters that behaved **curiously**. What did they say or do?

Word	Definition	Challenge
darting	Moving suddenly and quickly.	Do some **darting** across the playground. Which sports involve **darting**?
defective	Not working, something is wrong.	Do you have anything at home that is **defective**? What happened to it?
derelict	Empty and in a bad condition because it has not been used or lived in for a long time.	Think of three other adjectives you would use to describe a **derelict** house.
descent	Moving down.	What things can you make a **descent** in or on?
dilapidated	Old and falling to pieces, not looked after.	Describe what a **dilapidated** shed, house or building that you know looks like.

Word	Definition	Challenge
dilemma	When it is hard to choose between things.	Ask someone in your family what they have **dilemmas** about.
dwindling	Getting less and less.	Look up **dwindling** in a thesaurus. Find a synonym that you know well and talk about how the two words are the same and different.
eavesdrop	When you listen secretly to what people are saying.	Try **eavesdropping** on a conversation. What can you find out?
euphoric	You are really, really happy and excited.	You were **euphoric** after watching a match. What happened in the match?
exertion	Physical or mental effort.	What is the most **exertion** that you have ever done?

Word	Definition	Challenge
famished	Very hungry.	Slip the word **famished** into conversation with a class-mate or family member and see if they notice.
fascinated	You are really interested in something and you keep thinking about it.	What things are you **fasci-nated** by?
ferocious	A ferocious animal, person, or action is very fierce and violent.	Without telling people at home what the word is, make up clues and see if they can guess.
flabbergasted	Extremely surprised.	Look up the word **flabber-gasted** in the thesaurus. What other words are a bit like it? Talk to someone in your family about how the two words are different.
fleeting	It only lasts for a very short time.	Looking at someone so **fleetingly** that they do not even notice. Tell them afterwards!

Word	Definition	Challenge
flinch	If you flinch, you make a small sudden movement, especially when something surprises you or hurts you.	At the doctors you might **flinch**. Why?
flourish	To grow or develop successfully.	If plants are going to **flourish**, what do they need? If a child is going to **flourish**, what do they need?
frail	Not very strong or healthy.	Who do you know who is **frail**? Are there any characters from books who are **frail**?
fuming	Very cross.	What things make you **fume**?
furnace	A container or enclosed space in which a very hot fire is made, for example to melt metal, burn rubbish, or produce steam.	Where might you see a **furnace**? Why do we need **furnaces**?

Word	Definition	Challenge
gnaw	Keep biting at something.	Think of three animals which **gnaw**. What do they **gnaw** on?
haphazard	Something hasn't been organised or planned well.	Slip **haphazard** into conversation with a classmate or family member and see if they notice.
illuminated	Lit up, usually by electric lighting.	At night-time see if you can spot any buildings or places which are **illuminated**. What do they look like?
impression	What you think something, or someone is like.	What was your first **impression** of your current teacher?
impulsive	Do something quickly without thinking it through.	Talk to others at home when you have all been **impulsive**. What happened?

Word	Definition	Challenge
incognito	In disguise.	What fictional characters go **incognito**?
incredulous	You can't believe something because it is very surprising or shocking.	Think of something that others might say, 'I'm **incredulous**!' about.
indulgent	You are very kind to someone, usually in a way that isn't good for them.	Who in your life **indulges** you sometimes? What do they do?
inherit	Money or a house that a person gives to others after they die.	Ask family members if they have ever **inherited** anything.
kerfuffle	A lot of argument, noisy activity or fuss.	Notice times in the day when there is **kerfuffle**. Is there ever any **kerfuffle** in the classroom or at mealtimes?

Word	Definition	Challenge
loomed	Something that is large or has an unclear shape, often frightening.	Pretend someone was **looming** over you. Talk about what you would see and how you would feel.
manicured	If something is **manicured** it is neatly trimmed or well cared for.	Look **manicured** up in the dictionary. Now talk to someone about what things can be described as **manicured**.
mayhem	There is mayhem when a situation is chaotic, people are confused and not following the rules.	If there was **mayhem** in the classroom what would you see?
menacing	Someone or something that gives you a feeling that they are going to hurt you.	What fictional characters are **menacing**? What those characters do and look like?
miffed	A bit annoyed because someone did something you didn't like.	What makes your teacher **miffed**?

Word	Definition	Challenge
mischievous	To have fun by playing harmless tricks on people or doing things they are not supposed to do.	Invent a character who is **mischievous**. Describe them in detail. What do they look like, when and where do they live? What do they do that is **mischievous**?
monstrous	Being ugly and frightening like a monster.	If you saw a **monstrous** face, what would it look like?
motionless	Not moving.	When would it be a good time to be **motionless**?
mournful	Very sad. Sometimes because you have lost something or someone has died.	If someone is feeling **mournful**, what might you say to them? Why?
nourishing	Something that helps you grow or be healthy.	What foods are really **nourishing**?

Word	Definition	Challenge
ominous	Something that worries you because you think something bad is going to happen.	If the sky was **ominous**, what would it look like?
overlook	To not notice something.	Think of a time when you did something that your teacher **overlooked**.
overwhelming	Feelings or events that are too big to deal with.	Talk to someone about feeling **overwhelmed**. What things might **overwhelm** you?
perilous	Very dangerous. Something bad might happen.	Do you know any fictional characters who have gone on **perilous** journeys?
picturesque	Attractive and interesting and has no ugly modern buildings.	Where is the most **pictur-esque** place you have ever been? Describe what it was it like.

Word	Definition	Challenge
quirky	Something that is a bit odd. It isn't what you would expect.	**Quirky** is a bit like **weird**. Ask someone in your family to explain the difference between **quirky** and **weird**.
quiver	Shaking with small movements.	What feelings might you be having if you are **quivering**?
rancid	Food that has gone off, tastes bad and smells awful.	Imagine having to eat something **rancid**.
relentless	Something that never stops.	Slip **relentless** into conversation with a classmate or family member and see if they notice.
relics	Something which was made a long time ago. It is special in some way.	Where might you see a **relic**? Think about a **relic** that you have seen.

Word	Definition	Challenge
reluctantly	You do something even though you don't want to do it.	What things do you do **reluctantly**?
rouse	If someone **rouses** you when you are sleeping, they wake you up.	If you were going to **rouse** a family member early one day, what would you do?
rummage	Search for something in a rush and are be a bit careless with other things.	When was the last time you had to **rummage** for something in your bedroom? What did your room look like afterwards?
saunter	Walking slowly, in a casual way.	Ask someone to show you how they would **saunter**. Then you do it too. When is it good to **saunter**?
savouring	To enjoy an experience as much as you can.	Ask someone you live with, what things they like to **savour**.

Word	Definition	Challenge
scowl	To make an angry face. You don't say anything.	Who in your family **scowls**? What makes them **scowl**?
seething	To be really angry and you don't tell anyone.	The teacher walked into the classroom and you could see that she was **seething**. She was so angry. What would she look like?
skeletal	So thin that you can see bones through the skin.	What might have happened to a horse that is **skeletal**?
skirmish	A small battle	Imagine there was a **skirmish** in your street. What would cause it? What would it look like?
slapdash	If you are **slapdash** you do it without thinking or planning and you do not take care.	What would **slapdash** homework look like? What would you look like if the way you got dressed was **slapdash**?

Word	Definition	Challenge
slumber	Sleep.	**Slumber** and sleep are very similar, but when is **slumber** better to use? Talk to family members about this.
smouldering	A fire burning slowly without flame, usually giving off smoke.	Look **smouldering** up in a dictionary. Check that it matches your understanding of the word. Are there any slightly different meanings?
solitary	On your own.	When is it nice to be **solitary**? When isn't it?
stupendous	Extremely impressive or big.	Think of three things that can be **stupendous**.
suspicious	Not trusting someone or something.	If someone is being **suspicious**, what might you notice?

Word	Definition	Challenge
sway	Move slowly side to side.	What in nature **sways**? When do people **sway**?
synopsis	A summary of a piece of work.	Provide a **synopsis** of a film you have watched recently.
tentative	Being careful and unconfident because you are uncertain or afraid.	When is it good to be **tentative**?
tranquil	Calm and peaceful.	Imagine a **tranquil** place. What would you see and hear there?
treacherous	When something is dangerous and unpredictable.	Have you been somewhere or done something that was **treacherous**?

Word	Definition	Challenge
triumphantly	Doing something that shows you have won, or you have succeeded.	Pretend you are going to hold something up **triumphantly**. What would you be holding?
uproar	Lots of shouting and noise because people are very upset about something.	What might cause an **uproar** in your school?
venture	To go somewhere that might be dangerous.	What place would you like to **venture** to?
vibrant	Vibrant colours are very bright and clear.	What is the most **vibrant** piece of clothing that you own?
wrench	To pull or twist something very sharply.	Imagine a time when someone might **wrench** something from you. What would they **wrench** and why?

Word of the Week Introductory Instructions for Families

Word of the Week

To get children excited about words the whole school is starting 'Word of the Week.' Each week we will be displaying an interesting word and setting a small associated word challenge for you and your child. The challenges are small spoken tasks that do not require pen or paper. They just need you and some talk time, so easy to do on the way home or before bedtime. Get involved, have fun, and your child's vocabulary will grow!

Newsletter Ideas for Families

These are simple ideas that can be added to school newsletters or websites or sent to parents directly. The idea is to get them engaged in word learning and for children to have fun word learning at home too. For parents who speak other languages at home the key message is to play these games in their home language. The ideas listed are in no particular order. Mix and match and add your own, as long as your activities focus on word meaning as opposed to spelling.

Word facts and advice

1. As adults we need to know at least 30,000 words. Most of these words are learnt in childhood which means children need to learn seven new words every day. Reading to your child is one way to expose your child to more words. If you come across an interesting word in a book, try and use it again in a conversation with your child.

2. Talking is important. It is closely linked to reading, writing and learning. Did you know that research shows that spoken language abilities at 5 years of age predict their reading at 15? By playing simple speaking and listening games you may not think you are developing reading and writing, but you are. Get talking!

3. This one is for adults only! Listen to yourself when you talk to your child. Who does most of the talking? Who does the listening? Who asks the questions? Children's language develops more when adults follow the child's interests, use comments instead of questions and really show they are listening. Set yourself a little target such as: giving your child more time to answer, comment more and question less, talk about things that interest your child. It's not as easy as it sounds, but really worth the effort.

4. Keep on reading. Amidst the business of family life, it is hard to always find time to read to children. If you read to your child for 15 minutes per day, in a year they will have heard 1.5 million words. Reading slightly more challenging books to your child than they can read will help boost their reading too.

5. Words we think of as 'English' quite often originate from abroad. 'Ketchup' comes from Malaysia, 'bacon' is French, 'chocolate' is from Mexico, 'barbecue' from the Caribbean and 'pyjamas' come from India. Do you know where other words come from?

General ideas

1. Cooking. Do some cooking with your child. It involves co-operation, planning, reading, listening and lots of vocabulary – all skills you need to succeed in school, as well as being great skills for life. http://www.cookuk.co.uk/children-index.htm

2. Explore your local library. As well as books they will have audiobooks and events to develop speaking and listening. Your nearest library is at . . . (school to complete).

3. Make something with your child. It may be craft or construction. Doing it together gives lots of time for talking. Try and listen more than talk, and comment more than question. This website will give you further ideas, but you can do great things with bricks or by cutting up old cereal packets. bbc.co.uk/cbeebies/grownups

4. Linking up with school. Talk to your child's teacher to find out what topics are being taught in class. Ask them about any practical activities that are useful to support your child's learning. Supporting learning at home will really help your child to learn more about words they are learning in school. It might be as simple as a walk to the park looking for living things or a talking about what it was like when you were a child.

5. Reading and talking. Reading books to your child is a great way to develop your child's language. Books expose children to more complex language. For children who are learning to read, hearing stories can make them more enjoyable. For confident readers talk about what you have read together to further develop their understanding.

6. Get your child involved in planning parties or trips. This involves lots of talking, thinking and planning. 'Who will be coming? What will you need to do? What food will you need? What can you do before? Who needs to do what?' And maybe even 'How can we keep costs down?'

7. Asking 'Why?' Children like to ask 'Why?' so try asking some back. Start off with some obvious ones (usually related to 'rules') such as 'why do we need to look both ways before we cross the road?', before making it harder with more abstract ones like 'Why do our bodies like us to eat breakfast?' to ones that require real reasoning and opinions such as 'Which is better, to have holidays in summer or winter? Why?'

8. Presents. When thinking of presents for your child, think about how they stimulate talking. Board games or card games or creative play often involve lots of speaking and listening skills. Better than anything you can buy is the precious commodity of time with interested adults, like you. For your child's birthday give them some one to one time with you. No phone, no device, just you.

9. When listening to your child talking, once in a while comment when they use a great word. If they tend to use simple words, then show them how they could use more advanced words.

Specific word games

1. 'I spy'. 'I spy' is a familiar game, but it is great for learning language and phonics as well as filling in time on journeys. On the bus or in the car one player looks around and spots one item. They then give a clue 'I spy with my little eye, something beginning with' (and then say the letter). All other players guess.

2. Favourite movie. Ask your child to retell a favourite movie. If this is too long, start on something simpler like a favourite story book. Talk about the beginning, middle and end. Draw pictures of the main characters and use these to act out scenes.

3. One for the bus or car. Start with calling out 'a'. Everyone then tries to spot something that starts with an 'a'. When someone has called out an item starting with 'a' you can move on to 'b' and so on through the alphabet.

4. 'If I was king/queen for a day.' Ask your child 'If you were a king/queen for a day what would you do?' Give them some time to think of an answer, but once they have answered, ask them why they chose that action. Encourage your child to ask other people what they would do if they were king/queen for a day. A variation for older children is 'Prime Minister for a day'.

5. Team topic. On the bus or in the car, think of a topic and see how many things you can think of as a team in a set time. A minute might be enough. You can choose any topic but here are some ideas for inspiration: living things, things with wheels, things that make loud noises or things made of metal.

6. What's the same and what's different? Choose a topic that your child is interested in and ask them to select two items from that topic. Can they say what is the same and different about two things? For instance, comparing two TV shows or computer games. From *Harry Potter*, for example, it could be Sirius and Voldemort.

7. Change the story. Take turns to tell well-known stories with your child but make small changes to the story and see where that takes you. Change the character, the setting or the ending. You might have 'Big Red Riding Hood' or 'Goldilocks and the Three Kittens'. What would Big Red Riding Hood do to the wolf?

8. Build a story. One person starts a made-up story with one sentence, such as 'Once upon a time an enormous giant was sleeping when . . .' Other players then take turns to build on the story one sentence at a time. This is great to play in a group but is also fun when there are just two of you. Get creative and see what twists and turns you can add to your story. Add as much exciting vocabulary as you can.

9. Alphabet lists. Choose a category: it might be something like clothes, food or TV programmes. Then choose a letter. See how many words you can think of from that category that start with the target letter. e.g.: clothes starting with 's': scarf, socks, sweatshirt.

10. What does it do? This is another game for journeys: one player calls out an object that they see, and the next person tries to think of five things that it can do / that can be done with it. For instance: 'tree' – climb, chop, grow, fall down, and absorb carbon dioxide. If you are stuck indoors, you can look around you or in books and play the same activity. Younger children can just think of one or two things to do with an object.

11. Big brain. 'Big brain' is a variation on 'I spy' but rather than seeing something you need to think of an object and the letter it starts with. Great for playing when you are waiting somewhere. For instance: 'I think with my big brain something that is cold starts with an "I".'

12. Write down on pieces of paper a range of words. They might be related to what your child is learning in school or any words that they are familiar with. Place all the words in a 'hat'. Each person takes a turn at taking out words from the hat. The challenge is to describe the word without using it at all. For instance: for 'Africa' you can say it is a continent, giraffes live there, and you would find the River Nile there. Remember you can't say 'Africa' in the clue though.

13. Charades. Have fun acting out and guessing famous characters, films or books that your child is familiar with. Make sure you start with people, characters or topics your child is very familiar with.

14. What would you do? Think up small problems that your child might encounter such as getting lost, losing money, finding a mobile phone etc. Ask your child what would they do? Why? Ask other people what would they do and why. Which one is the best? Why? All of this is good practice with reasoning skills which are really important for lessons such as science as well as learning social skills.

15. Word associations. One player starts by saying a word. The next player says a word that is related to the first word. It can be related in any way. If another player cannot see how the words are related, they can challenge, and the connection needs to be explained. Keep going until a word is repeated or a connection cannot be explained. Here is an example: Egypt – Mummy – Dad – beard – Santa Claus – Christmas – trees – leaves.

16. Read a book or play together that has lots of direct speech (what people say) in it. If you don't have a book like this at home, your school or local library will have plays appropriate for children. Have fun making different voices and act it out as well.

17. 20 questions. One person thinks of an object. Others try and guess what it is by asking questions. The original player can only answer 'yes, no or maybe'. Give a clue if they are on the wrong track. Can they guess it in 20 questions?

18. I went shopping. This game is good for developing memory, so is good for adults too. One person starts by saying, 'I went shopping and I bought a . . .' (names a food item). The second player says, 'I went shopping and I bought . . .' and repeats the first player's item before adding their own. The third player continues saying the first two items before adding their own. And so on. See how many you can remember.

19. Ways to say. Brainstorm different ways of talking like 'mumbling, bellowing, whispering, croaking, and sobbing'. Check that all players know what they mean and have fun acting them out. Write the words on pieces of paper, scrunch them up and place them in a hat. Choose a simple phrase such as 'It's almost 4 o'clock.' Take turns taking a word from the hat, saying the phrase in that style, while others try to guess (and laugh!)

Vocabulary Within School Events

Turn the traditional school fair into a 'vocabulary fair' by adding words where you can; for instance, hold word challenges in which players must compete to name the most items in a category (e.g.: the highest number of food items in 30 seconds). Adding words to community events shows students and families that words are important in your school. More ideas provided below.

'Winning words' tombola

Make a list which contains engaging vocabulary, see below or use the list from page 43–79 for inspiration, and mundane words such as 'door', 'run' and 'green'. Print out both the interesting words and the boring words. Cut them out. Half of the interesting words and the set of boring words become the tickets.

Stick the other half of the interesting words to the prizes. Run as a normal tombola, but this one emphasises the point that good vocabulary wins prizes.

A full set of words can be printed from the companion website.

Boring words

door	train
run	office
green	time
water	school
room	line
bed	cake
game	purse

Interesting words

discover	discover
creep	creep
anxiously	anxiously
hopeful	hopeful
hurl	hurl
shriek	shriek
mysterious	mysterious

Photo booth

Make a photo booth frame and add words around the frame. Choose words like 'disguise', 'bold', 'quirky', 'dashing', 'old fashioned', 'stunning', 'funky', 'stylish', 'bold', 'hilarious'. Talk about the relevant words as you take children's pictures.

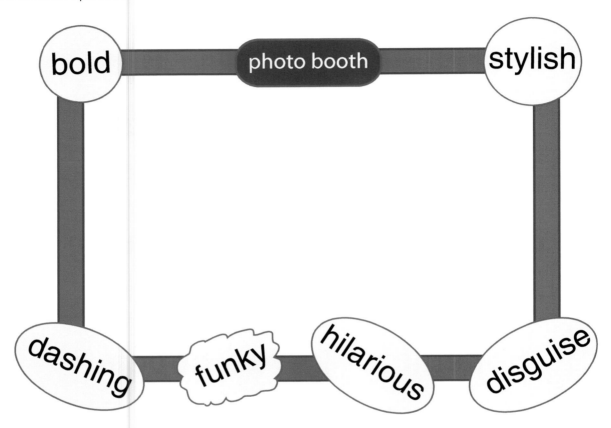

Digging for vocabulary treasure

Beforehand write words on pieces of card and roll them up. Use the list available via the companion website (examples on the following page, additional words on the companion website) or add your own. Secure with an elastic band. Hide this 'treasure' in a sand tray. On a display board write the list of words with some highlighted as prize winners.

Children then dig in the sand to find the 'treasure'. Once found, they match their written word to check if they have won a prize.

Adults should use the words during the activity. Try commenting on the words' meanings or using them in sentences e.g. 'Oh I'm **curious** about which prize you will get. I wonder what it will be' or 'We have lots of **tremendous** prizes on offer today. I bet you find that **tempting**.' The aim is for children to hear interesting words being used, rather than specific teaching, so have fun with it.

determined	determined
noticed	noticed
vibrant	vibrant
familiar	familiar
glimpse	glimpse
blazing	blazing
stunned	stunned

Word Wizard at a Halloween event

One adult dresses up as a Word Wizard for a Halloween event. Pin interesting words to his/her cloak. Children may either select from some examples below (additional words are downloadable from the companion website). Alternatively, they could write their own on blank pieces of paper. Thanks to Newton Primary School, Scotland for this idea.

repulsive	gobble
munch	gloomy

Community Events

Festival of words

Work with your local library and hold a 'festival of words'. This is a great way for your students to show their learning and engage others in word learning also. Here are a few ideas to get you started, but once again feel free to add your own innovations.

- Spoken word events: ranging from poetry recital to rap.

- Interactive displays: write and draw a favourite word or 'write a word I learnt from reading'. Children start it off, and library visitors add theirs too.

- Celebrate all languages: choose a few simple words and write or record how they are said in different languages. Share a story from a different culture.

- Old and new: students compare today's slang with older people's words from their childhoods.

- Tell a story about words: ask the librarian to read a book about words, such as *The Boy Who Loved Words* (Schotter & Potter, 2006) or *The Word Collector* (Reynolds, 2018).

- Invite families to any events and work to encourage other local schools to get involved too.

- Take photos and write blog posts of any events that can then be shared on school and library websites.

Class-Based

Reading

Promote reading

Independent reading is the most powerful activity that can be done to promote children's vocabulary (Beck et al., 2002). Encourage children to access a range of fiction and non-fiction books, graphic novels and magazines. Anything that gets them excited about reading will support long term vocabulary growth. Encourage parents to keep reading to their children well after children start reading on their own. Reading to children and talking about what they read will extend vocabulary and reading comprehension.

Audiobooks

Audio books and podcasts can be used to boost exposure to the spoken word as well. It also enables children to access stories with more complex vocabulary than they are able to read and is particularly valuable for children who are struggling to read fluently. Encourage children to listen to unabridged versions as these will contain more varied vocabulary.

The National Literacy Trust have produced a document 'Audiobooks and literacy: A rapid review of the literature' which includes the many benefits of listening to audiobooks.

Audiobooks are available via most public libraries and many mainstream publishers will offer some free titles, but other sources of free or cheap audiobooks include:

- getepic.com
- calibre.org.uk
- listening-books.org.uk
- librivox.org

Borrowbox: families can access audiobooks from libraries for free. Often users never need to even go to a library; it can all be done online. Download the 'Borrowbox' app to download eBooks and audiobooks. Users still need a library card number and their local library needs to be signed up to the scheme. Other options may be available.

Reading aloud

Select class books that include appropriately challenging, interesting and useful vocabulary. The daily reading aloud to children exposes less confident readers to more literate vocabulary, but it also gives the whole class the opportunity for discussion about words. Fiction is great but also interesting facts can engage a variety of children, so look at non-fiction too.

Authors' words

Jointly appreciating authors' use of vocabulary. When sharing a book with children ask, 'What words did you like?'

Suitably challenging vocabulary

All adults in the classroom should take great care in using appropriately challenging vocabulary. Use a wider range of words, but ensure they are still at the right level. The aim is to inspire, rather than overwhelm.

The 'Gift of Words'

Collecting powerful vocabulary and phrases from books as they are encountered is what Scott and Nagy (in Graves, 2009) call the 'Gift of Words'. They describe a process in which words and phrases from children's literature are collected and then discussed and displayed. Once a bank has been gathered children are then given opportunities to use the original authors' writing as a scaffold. For example, a child adapted 'She was a great potato of a woman' into 'He was a long string bean of a man.'

Draw your favourite word

Read a passage or story to the class. Ask them to identify and then draw one word that they liked. They may also write or say why they liked that word.

I liked the word **stifling**. It reminds me of how it felt last summer, when it was so hot you couldn't breathe.

Why that word?

When reading a shared text, select a word and discuss why the author has selected that word specifically. Ask children to justify their answers, for example, '"James climbed the ladder with **trepidation**." I think that **trepidation** was a good word to use because he must have been scared to go up the ladder and he also did not know what he would find when he got to the top.'

Story connections

After reading a story, choose key words from the text and write them on separate pieces of card. Instruct groups of children to discuss how the words are related to the story. They may also re-tell the story incorporating those particular words. For instance, the words **appearance** and **intimidating** could be highlighted for older children re-telling the story of 'Little Red Riding Hood' (based on ideas from Scott et al., 2008)

Important words

This works well with non-fiction texts. Give children photocopies of a short text on a topic and some marker pens. Ask them to highlight the words in the text that are important to the topic and convey information. Small groups may then compare and discuss their answers.

'Word Collector' bookmarks

Encourage children to write down interesting words that they encounter when they read. Chat about interesting and rare words but spend more time on really useful words. Talk about why children like their chosen words. Could any become words that the whole class can learn? You can also relate this work to the book *The Word Collector* (Reynolds, 2018). Use the 'Word Collector' bookmarks to write down interesting words that children would like to find out more about. To allow children to write on them the bookmarks should be printed on card and not laminated.

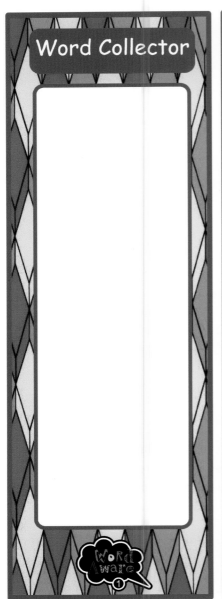  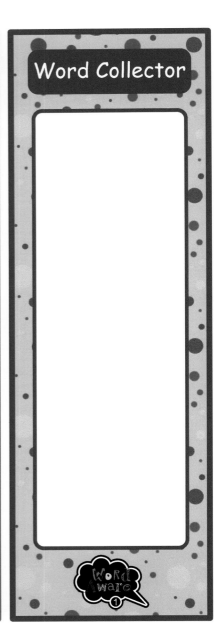

A printable version is available from the companion website.

'Finding different words' bookmark

Provide children with the 'Finding different words' bookmark that has a range of vocabulary-related tasks on it. This can be sent home as a task for parents to get involved with. A printable version is available from the companion website.

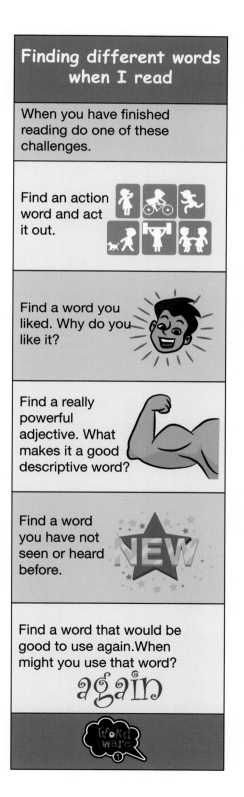

My treasure chest words

Name ....

When you find a word you like, write it here.

Date ....

Word that I like	Where I found it	Write the sentence that it was in	I like this word because ...

Keep listening out for the words that you like so you can learn more about them and start to use them!

Spoken language

Talk about words

The simplest of starting points. Talk about the importance of vocabulary. Highlight key vocabulary across all subject areas. Show your enjoyment of words. Make it contagious.

Ooh la la!

Rewarding students' use of powerful vocabulary. Fran Barber, a teacher from Steam Mills Primary School, rewards her students with a whole class 'Ooh la la!' when a particularly powerful word is spoken or written.

Words in motion

When starting a hands-on project (for instance, before a cooking or craft activity) talk about the key words that will be used. For younger children, expanding children's understanding of verbs can make a real difference. For older children the technical language is valuable for understanding instructions and explaining processes.

Cooking	Craft
pouring, sift, kneading, whisking, bake, grate, grease, melt, weigh, slice, spread, boil, fry, roll, simmer, peel, pour, chop, dip, pinch, serve, level, layer, beat, knead, mould, savouring.	connect, separate, assemble, carving, construct, dying, engraving, stitching, designing, knitting, organising, welding, produced, rubbing, showcasing, displaying, finalising, stencilling, wove, whittling, blended, bonding, embroider.

Model words

When children are feeding back about an object they have made, encourage them to use specific vocabulary.

> When you are telling me about how you made your model, I want you to use the word **connected**.

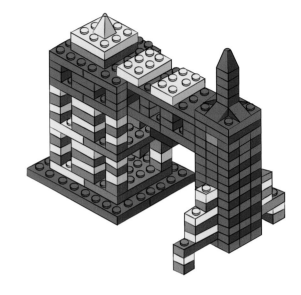

Artwork description

Look at a range of artworks that the class has completed. Encourage children to suggest adjectives that can be used to describe one of the artworks. Write these on the board. Teaching staff should then add a few more advanced adjectives. Children then take turns to select an adjective, nominate several artworks that fit that description and explain why.

Champion words

A challenge is set for the class. It might be to think of the best word to describe an object such as a volcano, how a character in a story might feel at a particular time or words to describe how someone is walking. Groups of children then brainstorm their ideas and each group nominates one word and a reason why. The chosen word is then added to a 'Champion Words' board. A printable version of the 'Champion Words' poster is on the next page and is available from the companion website.

What are the best words that describe the character's feelings? Which is the champion word?

Champion Words

CELEBRATING WORDS

Trips

Trips also often include exposure to new terminology. Prompt children to look out for and ask about new words. Trip destinations are often full of intriguing items. Take a moment to look at one and think of adjectives to describe it. Identify new words that you are going to encounter but remember to target really useful words that will be able to be used again. Adults accompanying the group and venue staff can then talk with the children whenever the target word is pertinent. E.g.: before going to the theatre think of related words such as **performance**, **interval**, **usher**, **actor** or **set**.

Writing

Sparkling vocabulary

Add 'jewels' on sparkling vocabulary. Any flat, sparkly sticker will do. This is a great quick win and boys seem to respond as well as girls.

The old man hobbled along the road

Words I like

Instruct children to read each other's work and select vocabulary that they like. Talk about why they like it.

Spice it up

Children can edit each other's work with the specific intention of choosing better vocabulary. Look for bland words like **said, went, walked, nice, lovely** and 'spice them up' with more powerful and evocative vocabulary. Compare the result with the original.

Writing warm-ups

Before starting writing, think about the sorts of words you could use. The 'Words Words Words' and 'All Sorts of Words' sheets on pages x and x can be used to help generate a variety of words. Printable versions are available from the companion website.

Words Words Words

Name: .... Date: ....

Look at the picture or read the text. Can you think of words linked to it?
Write down words in each of the categories.

Words for how the character is talking	**Words to describe feelings**
Any other words?	**Words to talk about how the character walks or moves**
Words to describe what the character looks like	**Words to describe the setting**

CELEBRATING WORDS

All Sorts of Words

Name: .... Date: ....

Nouns	Verbs

Topic, setting or character:

_____

Think about words that you could use when you are thinking about this topic, character or setting. Add your words into the right box.

Adjectives (words to describe something or someone)	Adverbs (words to describe **how** something is done, e.g. slowly)

CELEBRATING WORDS

Make your own riddles

Constructing riddles requires flexible thinking, but it can be done once a structure has been provided. The steps are as follows:

1. Think of a common object such as a school bag.

2. Describe what it looks like and what it does (carry it to school, zip it, has a handle, straps, made of fabric).

3. Convert to the following format:

   I can ... but do not ...

   I ... but cannot ...

   I ... but am not ...

4. What am I?

   Example:

   I go to school but do not learn.

   I am made of fabric but cannot be worn.

   I have a handle but am not a door.

   What am I?

   I am a bag.

Riddles can be made into flap books with clues on the front and answers underneath the lift-up flap.

Jokes

This is quite a high-level skill and children need to have a wide vocabulary, but of course it is also great fun. To generate jokes the steps are as follows:

1. Think of a subject, animal or person, for example, a dog.

2. Think of items associated with that subject, for example, bone, bark, tail, walk.

3. Select one of those words, such as bark.

4. Take off the first letter of that word, i.e.: ark.

5. Think of other words that start with this, for example, archangel, archaeologists. We will call this the new word.

6. Make up a reason for the original word and the new word to link, for example, dogs and archaeologists are related to bones.

7. Add on the old beginning to the new chosen word, ie barchaeologist.

Question: What do you call a dog that digs up old bones?

Answer: A barchaeologist.

(From Beck et al., 2002)

Analogies

Analogies often require in-depth knowledge, so solving them and generating them is a great language task. Start off solving simple noun analogies such as 'puppy is to dog as kitten is to . . .' before moving onto adjectives such as 'graceful is to clumsy as hot is to . . .'

Analogies

Name: .... Date: ....

Gram is to kilogram as centimetre is to	_____
Trees are to Christmas as eggs are to	_____
Apples are to fruit as leeks are to	_____
Swans are to birds as goldfish are to	_____
Light is to feather as heavy is to	_____
Sweet is to sugar as sour is to	_____
Tree is to leaf as flower is to	_____
Hammer is to nail as comb is to	_____
White is to black as up is to	_____

Short is to long as light is to	_____
Bees are to hive as people are to	_____
Chef is to food as artist is to	_____
Like is to love as dislike is to	_____
Moon is to night as sun is to	_____
Feather is to bird as fur is to	_____
Grey is to black as pink is to	_____
Hot is to oven as cold is to	_____
Petrol is to car as electricity is to	_____
Smile is to frown as pretty is to	_____
Cow is to mammal as snake is to	_____

Examples taken from:
https://www.teachervision.com/solving-analogies, https://examples.yourdictionary.com/analogy-ex.html,
https://examples.yourdictionary.com/analogy-examples-for-kids.html

Definition carousel

Each group starts with a big piece of paper. A different word is written in the middle of each piece of paper. Groups write what they know about their word. The papers are then exchanged, and the next group writes more before passing it on again. The fourth group collates the answers into a definition that can then be read and displayed.

Adjectives in a row

Source a number of adjectives, either from a thesaurus or a class brainstorm. They should relate to one attribute such as temperature, height, emotions, weight, light, types of rain, wealth, speed or size. You will need at least three, but you could do up to seven or eight. Write each on card and give one to each of a group of children. As a class discuss the order the children should stand in. The relationships are often not strictly linear, so encourage debate, and in particular children's reasoning, as this will help to refine thinking. To make a display the cards can be attached to a washing line. A selection is given on the next page.

chilly	cool	glacial		scorching	sweltering	hot	tepid	warm
small	tiny	minute	microscopic	average	little	petite	miniscule	
big	huge	medium	enormous	gigantic	colossal	vast	large	
rain	drizzle	shower	thunder-storm	downpour	sprinkle	dry	monsoon	
rich	wealthy	stinking rich	loaded	comfortable	prosperous	well-heeled	moneyed	
fast	quick	rapid	hasty	speedy	brisk	swift	nimble	
slow	sluggish	unhurried	relaxed	dawdling	leisurely	plodding	creeping	

Synonym triangle

Draw a triangle, as below. Write three synonyms, one at each apex. Within the triangle write in one colour how the words are all related. In another colour write along the perimeter how they are different. As well as looking the words up in dictionaries it is often useful to talk to a number of people to really get a good idea about the nuances. The list below will help get you started. See below for an example.

entertaining	absurd	hilarious
snivelling	sobbing	whimpering
adore	cherish	admire
riot	strike	boycott
sloppy	negligent	forgetful
outstanding	brilliant	remarkable
heartless	unsympathetic	callous

Synonym triangle example

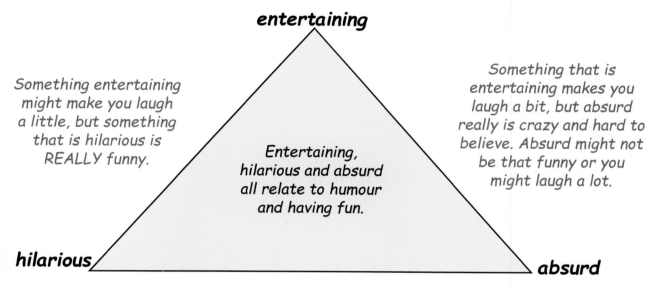

entertaining

Something entertaining
might make you laugh
a little, but something
that is hilarious is
REALLY funny.

Something that is
entertaining makes you
laugh a bit, but absurd
really is crazy and hard to
believe. Absurd might not
be that funny or you
might laugh a lot.

Entertaining,
hilarious and absurd
all relate to humour
and having fun.

hilarious

absurd

Absurd things are crazy, but
hilarious things are really just things
that make you laugh.

Linking words

The purpose of this activity is for children to connect words they know in lots of different ways to form phrases which can later be built into sentences.

Write a word in the middle of a 'sun'. If the chosen word is a noun, then select verbs to go around the sun's rays. For instance, if the selected noun is 'dog', possible verbs include 'leap', 'bark', 'wag', 'chew', 'snarl', 'yap', 'growl', 'lick' and 'bite'.

The opposite process can also be done. Select a verb such as 'soar' and write it in the middle of the sun, then write linked nouns along the sun's rays. For 'soar' the selected nouns could be 'hawk', 'bird', 'plane', 'prices', 'heart', 'emotions' and 'eagle'.

Similar linking can be completed between verbs and adverbs or nouns and adjectives. See the examples below. An extension to this task is for students to then write sentences containing the selected words.

Verb-noun example

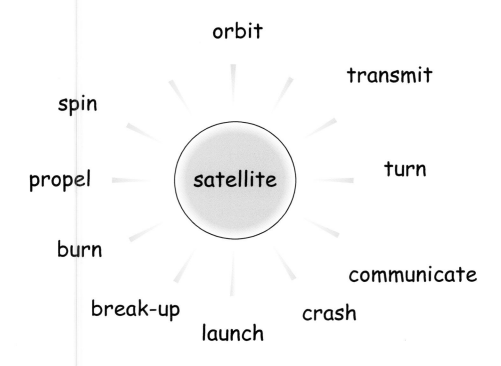

Suggestions to get you started

Identify verbs to go with these nouns	cat, chicken, farmer, grandad, lion, monkey, mouse, parrot, satellite, pipe, fabric, receptionist, performer, ink, professor.
Identify nouns to go with these verbs	cut, bend, eat, grow, make, sit, stretch, wash, collapse, understand, growl, float, exercise, recycle, raise.
Identify adverbs to go with these verbs	walk, dance, fly, speak, cry, sit, bang, whisper, listen, clap, curse, encourage, chop, disappear, glance.
Identify verbs to go with these adverbs	quickly, slowly, messily, beautifully, reluctantly, gracefully, wearily, dramatically, painfully, powerfully, kindly, unusually, clearly, precisely, randomly.

Identify nouns to go with these adjectives	sparkly, wide, dusty, flat, terrifying, adorable, uneven, interesting, comfortable, meaningless, antique, isolated, chubby, encouraging, rugged.
Identify adjectives to go with these nouns	ball, moon, tunnel, cornflakes, panther, owl, book, peanuts, grasshopper, politician, leader, toddler, victim, landscape, future.

Semantic feature analysis

Draw a table, writing a list of words in the left-hand column and the features to be analysed across the top. For instance, if analysing mini-beasts, the features you may wish to choose might be: fly, have six legs, live in large groups. This type of analysis works for:

Mammals, birds, dinosaurs, plants, furniture, food chain, shapes, properties, rocks, buildings, habitats, climactic zones, historical periods, mini-beasts, planets.

Example for common animals:

	Has a tail	Can swim	Can walk	Can fly
fish	✔	✔	✘	✘
bear	✔	✔	✔	✘
cat	✔	✘	✔	✘
bird	✔	✘ / ✔	✔	✔

Example for solar system:

	Source of light	In our solar system	Orbits around the sun	Supports known life
Sun	✔	✔	–	✘
Mercury	✘	✔	✔	✘
Earth	✘	✔	✔	✔
Moon	✘	✔	✘	✘
Stars	✔	✘ (apart from the sun)	✘	✘

Shape poems

Think of an object or animal, draw the outline of the item, brainstorm words related to the item and then arrange words around the shape of the object or animal. For instance, for 'dog', 'barking' could be emanating from its mouth and 'wag' near its tail. For 'gift', a box could be opening with words such as 'delight', 'glee' or 'disappointed' sprouting out, or written on the ribbons (from Scott et al., 2008).

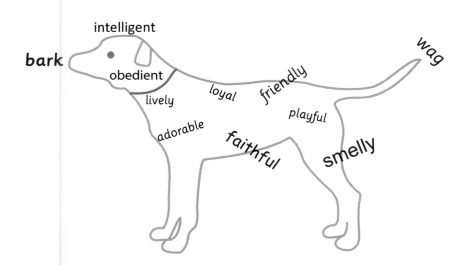

Cinquain poems

Cinquain poems define words, so help to reinforce vocabulary. They are quick and suitable for a wide range of ages. The 'rules' for the poem are:

Line 1: A noun

Line 2: Two adjectives about the noun

Line 3: Three verbs about the noun ending in -ing

Line 4: A phrase

Line 5: A synonym for the original noun

For example:

Traffic

Noisy, busy

Beeping, rushing, stopping

Not going anywhere

Cars

(From Scott et al., 2008.)

Pass on the picture

Give an interesting picture to each group of children. pobble365.com, literacyshed.com and onceup-onapicture.co.uk provide large selections. On a separate piece of paper each group writes words to describe the picture. Provide structure if needed. For instance, when describing a person, headings such as appearance, movement, speech and personality may be provided. 'Words Words Words' (page 100) or 'All Sorts of Words' (page 101) could be used for this exercise. Children are given a few minutes to write down their descriptive words before all pictures and written work are rotated to the next group. The process continues until all groups have worked on all pictures. The groups can then select the most powerful language for their picture. These can then be developed into written work or displays.

Descriptive word books

Groups of children together make a book of descriptive words. On the cover they write and draw a noun. The group brainstorms adjectives that describe that noun. Each child is allocated an adjective and writes an accompanying sentence which highlights the meaning of the adjective. This is then collated into a book.

Example: **Snake**

Adjectives	Sentences
• **Sinister** • **Flexible** • **Scaly** • **Dangerous** • **Sinister**	• The **sinister** snake moved silently towards its prey. • The **flexible** snake can bend and stretch through small gaps. • The **scaly** snakeskin is a beautiful pattern. • The **dangerous** snake is out to get you. • The snake slithers along looking **sinister**. You know something bad is going to happen.

Things to describe:

Animals: snakes, puppies, dinosaurs, dragons, spiders, penguins, kingfishers.

Book characters: Harry Potter, Matilda, Percy Jackson, Horrid Henry.

Story settings: use pictures of settings to inspire children. See pobble365.com, literacyshed.com and onceuponapicture.co.uk for inspiration.

Displays

Picture this

Prominently labelling vocabulary on regular displays or creating vocabulary-specific displays, such as words used to describe a volcano or how a person moves. Use images attached to the word to aid understanding. Communicate in Print (www.widgit.com) or Boardmaker (www.mayer-johnson.com) can be useful for this. Twinkl Create (www.twinkl.co.uk/create/app) and ARASAAC (http://www.arasaac.org/) are both free but offer comparatively limited range of images.

Photo challenges

Send a word home and encourage children to find pictures that exemplify the word. These can be photos children take or images from the internet. Back in school these can be displayed and discussed.

Examples:

Adjectives: hollow, quirky, dilapidated, frail, colossal, mournful, euphoric, picturesque, automatic, blaring, courageous, irritating, memorable, pristine, rewarding.

Verbs: bounce, hear, communicate, cruise, regret, collect, observe, squash, disagree, expand, hesitate, protect, repair, settle, wish.

My favourite word

Family members and staff bring in photos of themselves holding the 'Favourite Word' poster (see next page for a template that can be sent home) or a piece of paper where they have written their favourite word. Words can be in any language. Make the photos into a display. A printable version is available from the companion website.

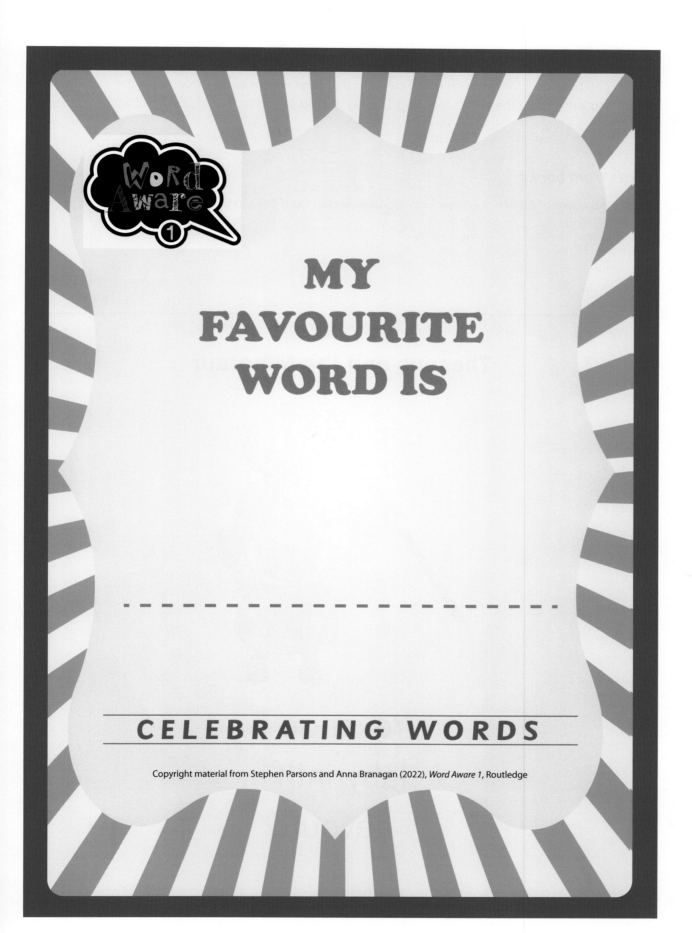

MY FAVOURITE WORD IS

CELEBRATING WORDS

Hidden meanings

Make a flap by folding over a piece of A4 card. On the cover write a word. Underneath the flap draw a picture and write about the word's meaning. Display at child height so that inquisitive children lift them up and find out more

Words from books

Display the cover of a book together with words selected from the story.

Words from

Theseus and the Minotaur

revenge

labyrinth

devour

Chapter mobile

For each book or chapter from the class book chose a selection of words and write these on card accompanied by an image. These can then be joined so that each book or chapter has its own mobile.

Definition mobile

Make a mobile by writing one word on a piece of larger card. Attach defining attributes such as descriptions, related words or key features (in word or picture form) on smaller pieces of card. Attach the smaller cards to the larger card with string to create a mobile.

Thesaurus on the wall

Display synonyms on the wall in a mind map style arrangement. Add pictures to increase its appeal. An example for 'emotions' is provided below.

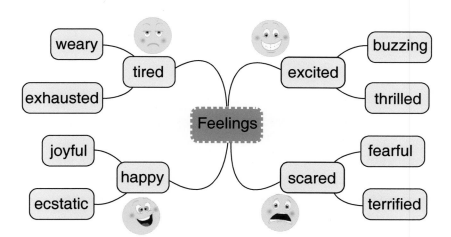

Descriptive vocabulary

Display interesting images such as those found at pobble365.com, literacyshed.com or onceupon-apicture.co.uk. Record children's suggested descriptive vocabulary on the board. A selection of the words can then be displayed around the printed image. In small groups or pairs children can be challenged to use the words in sentences.

Ways of talking

First of all, acknowledge that teaching children synonyms for 'said' is a challenging task. If it was straightforward, every student would take to it easily. For words to truly stick they require teaching time, as outlined in the next part of this book, but general exposure will help. There are many posters available online which we have collated at pinterest.co.uk/wordaware, but these may overwhelm the students they are designed to help. One option is to make it a 'living' display and talk about each word as it is added over a period of time. Encourage students to add the words as they encounter them, including the sentences they find the words in. The display may be subdivided into words which describe the sound of the speaking such as 'barked', 'hissed', 'grumbled' and 'murmured' and words which convey the speaker's intention such as 'revealed', 'reminded', 'argued', 'confirmed' and 'boasted'.

Craft activities

Making small craft items including the words that have been taught is a smart way to ensure that students continue to review words. Select activities which are fun to do, but also attractive to go back to and this will add to the joy of word learning. Some ideas to try include:

- One-word book, page 195.
- True or false folding books, page 198.
- Vocabulators, page 200.
- Magic books, page 202. These can be used for words that have been taught as part of a topic or as a general thesaurus (see below)

Personalised thesaurus

Make accessible thesauri to remind children to use more interesting synonyms for overused words such as 'said', 'like' and 'walk'. Magic books make great thesauri (page 203 has descriptions of how to make them or search YouTube for 'vocabulary foldable Martha Estorga' or 'cool vocabulary tools-foldables' for a video demonstration). Put boring words on the front, open up the book and write in more interesting options. Add more words as you learn them.

Paint chart thesaurus

An example of a paint chart thesaurus appears below. There are several more pages to print from on the companion website. Print onto strong card. Cut along the dotted line so you have four strips from each page. Punch a hole in the top left-hand corner and use a keyring to hold them altogether. The 'boring' word is given at the bottom. As children learn more interesting synonyms, they add these to the charts. Please see companion website to download printable versions.

like	pretty	walked	ran

Character slinkys

Think of a fictional character or historical character. Think of a number of adjectives to describe the selected individual. Edit these down to the best ones and add to the character slinky.

To make a character slinky. Cut a piece of card into quarters. Then fold the card in concertina style (like a fan). Open out the card so that there are now spaces to write. Add the words to describe the character. Attach head, arms and legs to the folded card.

obese
greedy
ginger
self-centred
powerful
wealthy
ruthless

Word Learning Resources

Give children access to a range of word learning resources such as dictionaries and thesauri. Students needs to be specifically taught how to use them but having them available at all times will ensure that they are integrated into everyday learning. Some schools place their word learning resources together and call them an 'information station'.

Dictionaries

The Collins COBUILD series provides straightforward, easy to comprehend definitions. There are several book versions available, starting with the COBUILD Primary Learner's Dictionary (2018). The online version available at www.collinsdictionary.com, provides similar, but more adult definitions on the first definition tab.

Online word learning tools

- wordhippo.com: particularly useful for synonyms, as it clearly delineates words with more than one meaning. This resource can also be useful for adults to help think of different ways of using a word. The sentences are a useful start for adults but need adapting for children.

- mathsisfun.com/definitions: visual dictionary maths vocabulary.

- lexipedia.com, visualthesaurus.com, visuwords.com: are all visual thesauri that present words in movable spider webs, so connections are visible. Fun to do, but primary/elementary students may need support to use meaningfully.

- liftlessons.co: a paid for site that the authors have been involved in which teaches key science vocabulary using short animations.

Books to promote and support vocabulary learning

- *Thesaurus Rex* by Laya Steinberg and Debbie Harter, 2003. An early children's book telling the adventures of a baby dinosaur using lots of synonyms.

- *Big Words for Little People* by Jamie Lee Curtis and Laura Cornell, 2008. An early years picture book which introduces children to the fun of big words.

- *Storyteller's Illustrated Dictionary* by Mrs Wordsmith, 2019. Wonderfully illustrated book defining a range of challenging words.

- *The Word Collector* by Peter H. Reynolds, 2018. A young children's book which tells the story of a boy who collects words. It has been read online by Barack and Michelle Obama, no less.

- *The Boy Who Loved Words* by Roni Schotter and Giselle Potter, 2006. A picture book with a similar plot to *The Word Collector*, but using more complex vocabulary.

- *Donovan's Word Jar* by Monalisa DeGross, 2018, is an early chapter book which tells a similar story to *The Word Collector*, about a boy's love of words.

- *Descriptosaurus* by Alison Wilcox, 2009. This is part of a series of reference books designed to model creative vocabulary for children aged 8 to 14 years.
- *Once Upon a Word* by Jess Zafarris, 2020. An often-humorous dictionary style introduction to the origins of words. For instance, 'ferret' originates from Old French for 'little thief'.

1.2 Word Games

The second component of 'Get Excited About Words' is word games. The message here is very simple: play words games and have fun. Word games give vocabulary a profile within the classroom, they motivate students and can also be used to review new vocabulary. Many word games utilise skills that involve exploring speech sounds and/or the meaning of a word, and so by playing word games students are also developing their word learning skills. Find games that you and your class like to play. Use the games suggested here or add your own. If adding your own, ensure they focus on the meaning of words and not just spelling.

Ways to use the listed word games:

• Make a regular slot in the class timetable to play vocabulary games. See 'Word Workshop' below.

• Keep games in mind that can be used whenever you have a few spare moments.

• Direct students who have completed their work ahead of their peers to independent learning activities.

• Send ideas home to parents. This extends word learning beyond the classroom. See page 317.

• Play a selection of games and add the most popular to a class compendium of word games. Once you have a repertoire, students can select games to play or be inspired to play them independently.

The ideas provided in this chapter generally need very little equipment and preparation, but it is worth taking note of a few favourites so you can recall them when you need to.

Word Workshop

Scheduling a brief 'word workshop' is a motivating and enjoyable way of reinforcing the words that the class has been learning that week as well as an opportunity to develop word learning skills.

Divide the class into groups of four to six students. Groups can all do the same activity, or each group can be given a different activity. Select vocabulary that you have been targeting in class. Write this on

the board or point the words out on the Working Word Wall, so that children are aware of the words that they will be focusing on.

Whole Class Games Requiring No Resources

These games require no resources and so are easy to use when you have a few moments to fill.

Henry VIII

Select a historical figure, fictional character or famous person who has featured in the class's learning. Work in groups to think of words that best describe this person or character. As a class refine these to the best five. Discuss how students made their judgements. Here are some examples:

Henry VIII: obese, greedy, self-centred, powerful and wealthy.

Red Riding Hood: kind, happy, helpful, innocent and naive.

An extension would be to draw a picture of the person or character and write the words to describe them.

Word chains

Select a category such as animals, food or things in the house. The first child writes a word on the board. The next child writes a word from the same category that starts with the last letter of the previous word, and so on. For example, antelop**e e**lephan**t t**ige**r r**hinocero**s s**loth.

I spy variations

Traditional 'I spy' is a great game to play, but these variations emphasise vocabulary more.

Variation 1: Thinking hat. Word meaning clues are given rather than letters and the object does not need to be within sight. Say, 'I put on my thinking hat and think of something that is (give a meaning clue).' If incorrect say, 'It's not that. I put on my thinking hat and think of something that is (original clue and a second clue).' Continue until the word has been guessed.

Variation 2: Big brain. In this game players give a clue containing the first speech sound of the word as well as a word meaning clue. As in 'thinking hat' players do not need to be able to see the item. For example, 'I think with my big brain, something that is part of a tree and begins with a "b".'

Gobbledygook

Read a sentence but miss out a word and instead say 'gobbledygook'. Encourage the children to guess the word. There may be several possible answers.

For example:

- 'The boy gobbledygooked down the road.'
- 'The girl ate a big gobbledygook.'

20 questions

Traditional game in which one person thinks of an object. Others try to guess what it is by asking questions. The original player can only answer 'yes', 'no' or 'maybe'. A clue may be given if the guessers are on the wrong track. Can the item be guessed in 20 questions? Keep a tally of the number of questions on the board.

What's the same and what's different?

Select two related words from a topic that the children are interested in and ask them to say what is the same and different about two things.

- Book or film characters, e.g. Superman and Batman, Sirius and Voldemort
- Sports, e.g. rugby and football, basketball and volleyball.
- Hobbies, e.g. different computer games, computer games and board games, reading and films
- Pop groups
- Restaurant chains, e.g. Nandos vs McDonalds

Alison is an acrobat in Asia

Starting at the beginning of the alphabet, the first player must generate a name, profession and place that all begin with that letter. For example, for the letter 'a': 'Alison is an acrobat in Asia'. The next player then has to do the letter 'b': 'Bob is a builder in Benidorm.' Make it more complex and add adjectives, so it becomes 'Alison is an ambitious acrobat in Asia.' To make it easier try name, food and a place in a house e.g. 'Alison is eating apples in the attic'.

Thanks to Julie Sanders, Pershore High School for this idea.

So many ways to talk and walk

Choose a common verb such as 'said', 'walk' or 'look'. Brainstorm or collect a range of more interesting words to replace the original word. Write these on the board, then carry out the related task below. Example words have also been provided.

	Task	Example words
Talk	Ask a child to pick a word and say 'I want a glass of water' in that manner. The other children are required to guess.	mumble, shout, rasp, mutter, yell, laugh, splutter, squawk, brag, giggle, sigh, remind, whimper, order, snarl, croak, suggest, complain, whisper, hiss, whine, croak, murmur, gulp, boast, beg, chirp, holler, boom, cry, weep, hesitate, squeak, order, screech, chuckle.
Walk	Ask a child to pick a word and then walk across the classroom in one of these ways.	stride, stumble, tiptoe, trundle, stomp, stroll, glide, strut, creep, amble, swagger, limp, waddle, dawdle.
Look	Act out as a group, e.g. 'Let's all rubberneck.' Discuss words that are very similar.	glance, stare, peep, flash, look daggers at, glare, gawp, scan, notice, rubberneck, glimpse, goggle.

Descriptosaurus (Wilcox, 2009) is a fantastic resource for descriptive language and will provide further inspiration for children aged 8 to 14.

Alphabet topic

Name a topic that the children are familiar with. Instruct all the children to write the alphabet vertically down the page omitting the letters Q, X and Z. The children are then required to write a word that belongs in that topic for each letter of the alphabet. An optional task is to write how the word is connected to the topic. This is a great independent task for children who have completed other work.

What am I?

For younger children, riddles need to be straightforward, rather than the conundrums
that older children enjoy so much. Three to four simple clues are usually adequate, for example:

- You find me . . .

- I can . . .

- An important thing about me is . . .

- When you look at me, you can see . . .

Reveal the object once it is guessed and repeat the clues to reinforce the learning.

For example: 'You find me in the kitchen. I can cook food. An important thing about me is that I get hot. When you look at me, you can see a handle and lid. I am a . . .'

A version of this game is available to download from the companion website.

Dictionary definitions

Divide the class into two groups. Distribute age-appropriate dictionaries so that all children have access to one. Group one starts reciting the alphabet until the other group tells them to stop. Group two then chooses a word from the dictionary that begins with that letter and also reads out the definition without using the target word. Group one guesses the word. Optional: group two give reasons why the guessed word is not correct. Points may be scored for correct guesses. (Thanks to Jill Goulding, Speech and Language Therapist, for this game.)

Games Needing Objects, Pictures or Printed Cards

Word spinner

Make a board spinner or purchase one (suggested online search terms: 'magnetic whiteboard spinner'). Attach it to the whiteboard and write letters or categories, such as 'animals', 'furniture', 'food' and 'clothing' around it. See below for further inspiration. Spin the spinner. When it stops, the children may either call out or write down items that belong to that category.

Make it harder by having two spinners, one for letters and the other for categories. Spin both at the same time. When they stop the children need to think of items in the category that begin with the letter shown. This makes a fun team game where the team has to think of five words.

Category cards are listed below and are also available to print via the companion website.

Animals	Clothes
Sports	Countries
Adjectives (describing words)	Boys'/girls' names
Things you can cut	Things you can smell
Somewhere you go on holiday	Things you would see at the zoo

Things that are cold	Things with legs
Food	Transport
Things that grow	Toys and games
Verbs (doing words)	Books
Things you can see at the seaside	Emotions
Things that are fast	Things that are red
Things in a classroom	Things that open
Furniture	Living things
Shops	Breakable objects
Things that are long	Things that make noise

Quick as you can

Print out the category cards above. Print out the alphabet cards on the next page. Printable versions are available from the companion website. See page i for details. Shuffle both packs and turn them face down. Turn over a letter and a category card. How many items can the group think of that start with that letter, from that category? Can be played in teams where the winner is the first team to write down five words which match the criteria. (Thanks to Julia Peters, Speech and Language Therapist, for this idea.)

a	b	c
d	e	f
g	h	i
j	k	l
m	n	o
p	r	s
t	u	v
w	y	

In the manner of the word . . .

This game targets adverbs. Either choose from the list below or with the class, generate four to six adverbs (e.g.: slowly, painfully, joyously, speedily, messily, quietly and sadly). Write them on the board. Ensure that all class members know the meaning of each word. Ask one student to leave the room. Pick one of the adverbs, such as **sadly**. The student who has left the room then comes back in and asks someone to act an everyday task in the 'manner of . . .', for example, **sadly**. 'Isaac, make a cup of tea **in the manner of the word**.' Isaac then acts making a cup of tea as **sadly** as he can. If the first child is unable to guess what the target adverb is then a different child is asked to do another task **in the manner of the word** – and as many other children as needed take turns until the answer is guessed. Once the first child guesses correctly, a second child goes out of the room and a different adverb is chosen. The child or children who are acting are permitted to talk. (From Nash, 2013)

Adverb examples

slowly, painfully, joyously, speedily, messily, quietly, sadly, energetically, crossly, loudly, dramatically, sternly, happily, sedately, reluctantly, solemly, gracefully, blindly, covertly, hastily, boldly, wildly, wisely, daintily, sleepily, thoughtfully, jokingly, proudly, suspiciously, rapidly, wearily, dejectedly, unexpectantly, shakily, sheepishly, rudely, elegantly, intensely.

'In the manner of . . .' tasks

Have a wash	**Ask your mum if you can go out and see a friend**
Pick some flowers and give them to someone	**Write 'the cat sat on the mat' on the board**

Get dressed	Brush your hair/teeth
Walk across the classroom	Dance
Have a conversation on the bus	Swim
Play in the park	Blow out candles and cut a birthday cake
Talk to someone on the phone	Buy an ice cream
Make a cup of tea	Have a drink in a coffee shop

Adverbs inspired by: https://7esl.com/list-of-adverbs/

Pass the object

Find an interesting object which has many features, for example an elephant or a toy train. Pass the object round the group. Each person says something to describe the object. For example, for **protractor**: 'It is a circle, it has degrees on it, used for measuring, has numbers, is made of plastic, it is transparent.' Extension: after a number of turns one child summarises all that has been said.

I give you this gift

For this activity some interesting objects are required. As a group, think about the words that can be used to describe objects. They might be about colour, size, texture or a specific attribute. Go around the group so each child has a turn at choosing an object from the bag. One child gives it to the next child using the phrase, 'I give you this (names object) because . . .' The sentence tells the person something about the object, for example, 'because it is **shiny**', or 'because it goes **fast**'. (From Nash, 2013.)

Love glove

Find an interesting glove. Explain that it is a 'love glove' and that it helps you to think of things that you love (or really like). Start by giving the group an example, such as 'I love to eat chocolate cake.' Pass the glove round with each child putting it on in turn and saying one thing they love. The first time around, let the children say the name of any item they love. After everyone has had a turn, choose a specific category for the group, e.g.: television shows, food, toys or games. Pass the glove round and encourage the children to name their favourite item in that category. (From Nash, 2013.)

'Reverse Taboo'

Use the cards from the commercially available game 'Taboo' (www.hasbro. com) or cut out the cards listed below. Alternatively, make your own by writing cards with target words and three closely related words. e.g., pyramid: Egypt, triangle, pharaoh. The rules of traditional 'Taboo' forbid the speaker from using certain words which are related to the target word. When playing 'Reverse Taboo' the speaker must give clues that include the words on the card (but still avoid the target word). It makes it much easier but is good for practising defining words as well as reviewing words.

(Thanks to Yildiz Katkin, Speech and Language Therapist, for this idea.)

Print the cards below onto stiff card. Cut along the horizontal lines so you have a 'domino' with one word on the left and three words on the right. Fold down the middle line and put all of the cards into a hat, or similar. The first player selects a card. Their task is to define the word on the left by using all three words on the right, but without saying the word on the left. The first player should use full sentences when using the three words. Other players cannot guess until all three words on the right have been used.

flower	smell pretty petals
dinosaur	extinct creature pre-historic
mountain	hill climb high
population	many place people
tree	branch grow leaves
planets	sun earth orbit

bear	furry grizzly polar
train	track ticket travel
ice-skating	cold blade dance
ticket	money cinema buy
brakes	stop car press
sun	warm light sky
banana	yellow peel eat
computer	keyboard screen internet
biscuit	tea crumble packet
umbrella	rain up windy

rocket	space travel astronaut
desert	sand hot Sahara
grandmother	woman old family
football	kick game net
lock	key door open
blanket	wrap warm fold
fridge	food shut cold
coffee	hot brown drink

What can it do?

Cut out the word cards below and overleaf and put in a container. The first player takes one word card out and the next person (or group of people) is required to think of five things that it can do or that can be done with it. For example, **tree**: climb, chop, grow, fall down and absorb carbon dioxide. Add your own word cards as well.

apple	**baby**
ball	**pencil**
penguin	**hand**
flower	**water**
lollipop stick	**rubber band**

wire	air
foot	leaf
cat	spoon

Emotions spin game

A whiteboard spinner is required for this game. Search online for 'magnetic whiteboard spinner' to see examples. The range of emojis is provided below but larger versions are available to print from the companion website which accompanies this book. Check all children know what the words mean. Arrange a mixture of six to eight positive and negative emotions in a circle around the spinner and give it a spin. When the spinner stops on an emotion word the children are asked to describe a time when they felt that way. A variation is to ask for examples of situations when characters from a shared text experienced that emotion or to think of a synonym for the emotion.

This resource is taken from *Language for Behaviour and Emotions* (Branagan, Cross & Parsons 2021)

Negative emotions					
afraid	afraid	cautious	terrified	threatened
embarrassed	ashamed	embarrassed	self-conscious	shy
sad	upset	disappointed	sad	grumpy
left out	excluded	left out	lonely	rejected
anger	angry	annoyed	irritated	frustrated
resistant	argumenta-tive	defensive	resentful	stubborn

stressed	overwhelmed	panic	stressed	tense
anxious	anxious	dread	nervous	worried
uneasy/ unsure/ confused	awkward	confused	uncomfortable	unsure
negative relationship related	controlled	hurt	jealous	needy
other	bored	disgusted	guilty	tired

Positive emotions	happy	cheerful	enjoy	happy	pleased
	caring	kind	caring	protective	gentle
	positive relationship feelings	co-operative	forgiving	loyal	generous
	confident	brave	confident	daring	
	content	calm	comfortable	relieved	safe
	looking forward	anticipation	expectant	hopeful	inspired

	excited				
		eager	excited		
	other	proud			
Other	interested	curious	interested	nosy	
	surprise	amazed	astonished	shocked	surprised

Hink pink

A 'hink pink' is a rhyming pair of words that together form the answer to a riddle. Each pair of words must have the same number of syllables. To generate and solve them requires a great deal of linguistic agility, so they are a fun way to develop vocabulary learning skills.

Use the resources on the next two pages (printable versions available from the companion website):

Variation 1: give out both hink pink clue and the answer and encourage children to match.

Variation 2: give out either the hink pink clue or the answer and see if they can work out the other half.

These are inspired by Beck et al. (2002) but many more are available if you search online for 'hink pink'.

An extension to this activity is for children to make up their own. To make up a hink pink first think of a rhyming adjective and noun. For example, 'fat' and 'cat'.

Then think of synonyms of the words:

Fat: large, obese, overweight

Cat: feline, pet

Then make up a question, the answer to which is the two rhyming words.

Q: Hink pink, what do you call an overweight feline?

A: A fat cat

Hink pink What do you call a rodent's home?	Answer mouse house
Hink pink What do you call a superior bird home?	Answer best nest
Hink pink What do you call an empty seat?	Answer bare chair
Hink pink What do you call a miserable father?	Answer sad dad
Hink pink What do you call a young person running free?	Answer wild child
Hink pink What do you call an incorrect tune?	Answer wrong song
Hink pink What do you call a nice gift?	Answer pleasant present
Hink pink What do you call a mad flower?	Answer crazy daisy
Hink pink What do you call a distant vehicle?	Answer far car

Hink pink What do you call a large branch?	Answer big twig
Hink pink What do you call a wealthy wizard woman?	Answer rich witch
Hink pink What do you call an insect that isn't wet?	Answer dry fly
Hink pink What do you call a bird that doesn't go fast?	Answer slow crow
Hink pink What do you call a tune that goes on and on?	Answer long song
Hink pink What do you call a tight-fitting carpet?	Answer snug rug
Hink pink What do you call a cloudy 24 hours?	Answer grey day
Hink pink What do you call a 50% giggle?	Answer half laugh
Hink pink What do you call a rabbit who tells jokes?	Answer funny bunny

References

Beck, I., McKeown, M. & Kucan, L. (2002). *Bringing Words to Life: Robust Vocabulary Instruction.* New York: Guilford Press.

Branagan, A., Cross, M. & Parsons, S. (2021). *Language for Behaviour and Emotions.* Abingdon, Oxon: Routledge.

Chiat, S. (2000). *Understanding Children with Language Problems.* Cambridge: Cambridge University Press.

Clark, E. (1993). *The Lexicon in Acquisition.* Cambridge: Cambridge University Press.

Collins COBUILD Primary Learner's Dictionary (2018). Glasgow: HarperCollins.

Curtis, J. L. & Cornell, L. (2008). *Big Words for Little People.* New York: HarperCollins.

DeGross, M. (2018). *Donovan's Word Jar.* New York: HarperCollins.

Nash, S. (Ed.) (2013). *Communication and Language Activities.* Banbury, Oxon: Hinton House.

National Literacy Trust (2020). https://cdn.literacytrust.org.uk/media/documents/Audiobooks_and_literacy_2020.pdf

Reynolds, P. H. (2018). *The Word Collector.* New York: Orchard Books.

Sanders, E. F. (2014). *Lost in Translation: An Illustrated Compendium of Untranslatable Words from Around the World.* London: Square Peg.

Schotter, R. & Potter, G. (2006). *The Boy Who Loved Words.* New York: Schwartz and Wade Books.

Scott, J. & Nagy, W. (2009). Developing word consciousness. In M. Graves (Ed.) *Essential Readings on Vocabulary Instruction.* Newark, DE: International Reading Association.

Scott, J., Skobel, B. & Wells, J. (2008). *The Word Conscious Classroom.* New York: Scholastic.

Steinberg, L. & Harter, D. (2003). *Thesaurus Rex.* Cambridge, MA: Barefoot Books.

Wilcox, A. (2009). *Descriptosaurus.* Abingdon, Oxon: Routledge.

Wordsmith, Mrs. (2019). *Storyteller's Illustrated Dictionary.* London: Mrs Wordsmith.

Zafarris, J. (2020). *Once Upon a Word.* Emeryville, CA: Rockville Press.

Step 2: Teach Words

Teach Words

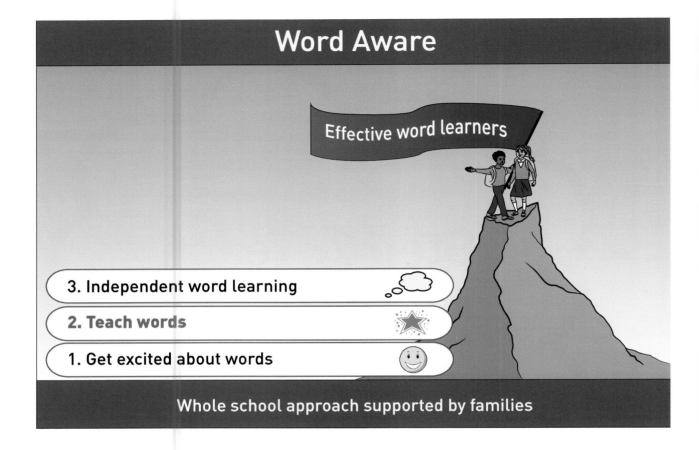

Introduction

Stage one of the *Word Aware* process was to create an excitement about words and build a vocabulary-rich environment in your school. This is an important and ongoing action which underpins vocabulary learning, but it is non-specific and reliant on students' innate skills to be successful. The first stage will ensure that students are engaged and interested in word learning, but the second phase, as outlined in this section of the book, focuses this energy on the words which are most important to learn.

Teaching words is something that happens in every school every day, but this section will outline how teaching can be refined and improved upon so that the words really 'stick'. The approach outlined applies vocabulary research in a practical manner to make word learning more effective for all students.

Over the past decade the authors have worked with educators in many schools across a number of countries and education systems. The most common vocabulary teaching issues include:

Word selection: where do I source words from? Which words should I choose?

The pace of the curriculum: the curriculum requires me to teach so many words. There is just no time to teach them all.

Retention:	so many of my students do not remember the words that they've been taught.
The 'Word Gap':	my students have such huge gaps in their vocabulary knowledge. Simple things I expect them to know, they have no idea about.
Applying their knowledge:	I have taught words, but then my students either do not use the words, or they use them incorrectly.
Vulnerable learners:	many of my students have adequate vocabulary, but a number of more vulnerable learners have poor vocabularies and cannot keep up, yet alone close the gap.

All of these issues are addressed by the approach outlined in this section of the book. However, direct teaching is never enough, and it is only one component of becoming an effective word learner. The authors strongly advocate that teaching words is used in conjunction with 'Step 1: Get Excited About Words' and 'Step 3: Independent Word Learning'. This provides children with a rich and varied range of word-learning opportunities.

Teach Words: The STAR Approach

This section introduces the specific teaching of vocabulary related to subject topics and whole class texts. The format for teaching words from both sources is carried out in the same fundamental way. The process is based on the work of Blachowicz and Fisher (2015). The acronym for the teaching process is STAR, which stands for:

Select
Teach
Activate
Review

Select

As there are a limited number of words that can be focused on for direct teaching it is important to choose words that will have the most impact.

Rather than being taught in one exposure, word knowledge develops as the word is encountered over time (Chiat, 2000). Therefore, it is important to choose words that are likely to be encountered again to ensure that a full knowledge of the word is built up. If rare words are taught, there is less likelihood that the words will be heard with enough frequency to be learnt in depth. It is therefore crucial that the right words are selected. If not the remainder of the STAR process is wasted.

The targeted words that are sourced from books or topics are sorted into three categories (Beck et al., 2002) with the middle group called 'Goldilocks' words (Stahl & Nagy, 2005). These are words that are not too easy, not too hard but just right. The main feature of these words is that they are really useful words that children will encounter again.

Teach

The teaching process is quick and simple. It is designed to fit within whole class teaching, and not to be an add-on. The aim is to start the word learning process so that full understanding can naturally develop as children encounter the word over time. In effect, the teach process is about highlighting which words are important and kickstarting the word learning process rather than teaching the word completely, and if done correctly this will happen naturally with limited further effort.

During the *Word Aware* 'teach' process the phonological (speech sound) and semantic (meaning) features of the selected word are identified and presented systematically. Clear definitions and links to the children's experiences are provided. Multi-sensory experiences, including actions and songs, are added to enable the child to remember the word. Finally, the new word is added to the Word Wall and Word Pot to facilitate its long-term retention.

Activate

During the activate stage children have the opportunity to bring the new word to life. To fully know a word, children need to be able to integrate the new word with their existing knowledge and understanding of the world. This is done by making explicit links to their understanding of the word. For instance, the word **prototype** can be activated by having discussions whilst the children build **prototypes** of products which they have designed. The children hear the new word in context, so they are building up a fuller understanding of the word. After learning the word **habitat,** the children then learn about the rabbit's **habitat** and build up a picture of what the **habitat** is like.

Activating words can also be facilitated by asking questions that require children to re-think their knowledge of the word, create new links and deepen understanding. Questions such as 'What does **reasonable** mean?' do not require deep thinking whereas 'Would you think it was **reasonable** if I asked you to read the whole book for homework tonight. Why or why not?' To access this type of activation question children must have well-developed language skills.

Review

'Review' is the final part of the process. The purpose is for children to encounter the target words again, in spoken or written form, thus continuing their learning. If children do not encounter words again the risk is that they are forgotten. The pace and episodic nature of much of the curriculum presents obstacles, as it focusses on the next topic and associated new words rather than looking back and embedding previous teaching. Our maxim is 'If it's worth doing, it's worth reviewing.' If words have been selected, taught and activated, it is crucial that they are then reviewed.

Time in class is pressured, so the activities provided are either quick whole class reviews or designed so that children will do them spontaneously and independently. Word Walls and Word Pots need to be part of the routine, but you can also use the creative ideas listed or any of your own. Review activities need to provide meaningful encounters with the words. Much better to have a thirty second discussion about when and where children experienced 'torrential' rain rather than send them off to find the letters 't-o-r-r-e-n-t-i-a-l' in a word search.

Teach Words: Applications of the STAR Approach

The STAR approach (select, teach, activate, review) can be applied in two different ways, as follows:

2.1	STAR Topic 	For vocabulary used in mathematics, science, geography and history, or any subjects in which there is a prescribed vocabulary to learn.

2.2	STAR Literacy	Applies to vocabulary that is encountered in whole class shared texts.

Eventually words need to be taught across the whole curriculum, but initially practitioners are recommended to start with one curriculum area and build confidence before extending it.
See 'Implementing Word Aware' (page 17) for further guidance about how to start with *Word Aware*.

2.1 Teach Words: STAR Topic

Select

Select: where to start

- Pick a Goldilocks word to teach. A word that is really useful and will be encountered again.

To get started with selecting which words to teach for your topic, identify the range of vocabulary needed for this topic. This can be from curriculum guidelines or from a list that is devised within your school. If using lists prepared by others it is advisable to check that the lists are complete and reflect the content that you intend to teach. The process of selection should be embedded into the topic planning process rather than an add-on. If it becomes just one part of the planning process it will not become burdensome.

Divide the words on your list into three categories. These categories are 'anchor' (everyday) words, 'Goldilocks' words (words that are not too easy and not too hard, but just right) and 'step on' words (words that are less likely to be encountered again). The table below describes the three types of words in full. Look at your list of topic words and divide them into the three categories using the table given on the next page.

Anchor words	Goldilocks words Not too easy and not too hard, but just right	Step on words 
Children have a thorough understanding of these words. Everyday spoken and written language for a child of this age. Used at home and in daily interactions. Children may have become familiar with this vocabulary through prior teaching.	**Really useful words** Likely to be encountered again in reading or oral language. Average adult has a **good** level of knowledge of the word. Words that are very topic specific but are core to the topic. Age 7+: Desirable for children to use in their writing.	Less likely to be encountered again in reading or oral language. Average adult does **not have much** knowledge of the word. Words that are particularly topic specific and are not core to the topic. Age 7+: Not a word that children usually need to use in their own writing.

If a child needs work on 'anchor' words then provide small group teaching or differentiated activities as well as whole class teaching for 'Goldilocks' words.	'Goldilocks' words will be the words that are taught to the whole class. Select one per lesson.	'Step on' words that are needed for comprehension can be briefly explained but are not the focus for in-depth teaching.

(Adapted from Stahl & Nagy, 2005 and Beck et al., 2002)

Select example

Age: *6–7 years*	**Subject:** *Science*	**Topic:** *Living things and their habitats*
Anchor words	**Goldilocks words** Not too easy and not too hard, but just right	**Step on words**
Children have a thorough understanding of these words. Everyday spoken and written language for a child of this age. Used at home and in daily interactions. Children may have become familiar with this vocabulary through prior teaching.	Really useful words Likely to be encountered again in reading or oral language. Average adult has a **good** level of knowledge of the word. Words that are very topic specific but are core to the topic. Age 7+: Desirable for children to use in their writing.	Less likely to be encountered again in reading or oral language. Average adult does **not have much** knowledge of the word. Words that are particularly topic specific and are not core to the topic. Age 7+: Not a word that children usually need to use in their own writing.
living *dead* *never* *sorting* *alive* *healthy* *plants* *animals* *ocean* *woodland*	*habitat* *food chain* *depend* *variety* *classify* *compare* *essential* *rainforest* *seashore*	*micro-habitats* *deciduous* *marine* *Galapagos* *grasslands* *coniferous*

Word categorisation is dependent on children's experiences, so words such as 'ocean', 'seashore', 'woodland' and 'grasslands' will all vary according to the school location and children's resultant experiences. The underlined words are the priority Goldilocks words to teach. The precise number chosen to be taught will depend on the length of topic and the teaching time available.

Beck et al.'s (2002) work is widely referenced either explicitly, or implicitly with the highlighting of 'Tier 2' words. We are great admirers of Beck et al.'s work but have tweaked their categorisation because their processes work well for Literacy/Language Arts but do not apply well to other curriculum areas. Under Beck et al.'s framework almost all technical vocabulary is classed as Tier 3, and thus there is no prioritisation of words within mathematics, science, geography or history.

There will be some variation about how to categorise words. It is important to think about the children you are working with as their vocabularies will reflect their experience and skills.

Further examples of identifying 'Goldilocks' words are on pages 156 to 157. A blank copy to use for planning is available on page 206.

Select one 'Goldilocks' word for every lesson that topic is taught. All of the words in the above table are going to be encountered as part of the topic, as we still want to expose children to rich vocabulary, but the quality teaching time should be spent on the 'Goldilocks' words so that children's knowledge can be deepened. It is tempting to try and teach lots of words as there are so many words that children need to know to access the curriculum. The risk in doing this is that children end up with superficial knowledge of many words, and a full understanding of few.

The very definition of 'Goldilocks' words means that children are going to encounter these words again in other situations. Many of the words are cross-curricular and children will come across them outside of school also. Once an initial outline of a new word is sketched via direct teaching, natural exposure to the word in different contexts will over time fully establish the word. Choose the right word and the natural word learning process will carry students forward.

Once you have a number of 'Goldilocks' words, look through the list and identify which words are key to the topic. Select one for each lesson. If it is a six-week topic that is taught once a week then six words should be identified. The word should be linked to the content that is being covered that week as this enables natural reinforcement of the word. In the above example the underlined words are considered to be the priority 'Goldilocks' words to teach.

Sometimes there are words that are very topic-specific and only occur in relation to a particular topic. These words may be so central to the topic that it cannot be discussed without understanding them. For example, when learning about nutrition it is essential to learn about **carbohydrates**. Although less likely to be encountered outside that topic, they will be regularly used within it and so these words can be classified as 'Goldilocks' words.

Don't teach opposites in the same lesson.

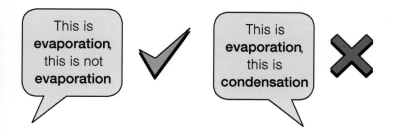

Traditionally, words that are opposites are often taught together. For instance, the words **evaporation** and **condensation** are often introduced in the same lesson. When both terms are new to the class, the labels may be learnt but may not be attached securely to the corresponding meaning. The result is a muddled, partially correct, partially incorrect understanding of each word. Once confused, it may take considerable effort for children to then work out which is which.

It is better to introduce one concept at a time and make sure the first is established before introducing the other. If the opposite term needs to be used, it can be described with a negative, for example, 'This is **evaporation,** and this is **not evaporation**.'

Once one concept has been established then the opposite term can be easily introduced as much of the conceptual learning has already been completed. When to introduce the second word depends on a number of factors such as prior knowledge, abstractness of the concept and children's word learning skills, and so it is hard to give a definitive answer. However, care should still be taken not to introduce the second concept too quickly.

Once the first word has been firmly established, then both opposites can be used together naturally. Care just needs to be taken during the early teaching phase. After that you can relax and use the terms naturally.

Opposites are the words most likely to be confused, but occasionally there are other topic words that are taught together which may get confused. 'Orbit' and 'rotate' both relate to how planets move and so there is potential for confusion between them as well, so the same caution applies.

 There will be some children with significant word learning difficulties who, for a variety of reasons, will not have a thorough understanding of 'anchor' words. These children can be included in the whole class teaching of 'Goldilocks' words but they will need additional teaching of 'anchor' words. This can be done individually, in small groups or by involving families.

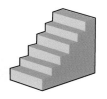 'Step on' words should still be used within the classroom as they are a significant part of the curriculum but should not be specifically taught to the whole class. Whole class teaching time is precious and so should concentrate on the words that will really make a difference to the whole class. 'Step on' words often add interest to the topic and so some children may like to learn more about them and that should not be inhibited. As they are not key to understanding the topic, a superficial knowledge is enough, and so a quick mention and explanation is all that is needed.

Select examples

Subject	Age group	Topic	Anchor	Goldilocks	Step on
Geography	6–7	Geographical skills and framework	*island* *land* *map* *distance*	*country* *continent* *compass* *atlas* *landmark* *co-ordinates*	*Ordnance Survey maps* *grid reference GIS (geographical information system)*
Science	7–8	Nutrition	*bones* *sugar* *bread* *eggs* *rice* *potato* *pasta* *fruit* *vegetables* *water* *meat* *fish*	*balanced diet* *carbohydrates* *dietary fibre* *fats* *protein* *food types* *dairy* *vitamins* *minerals* *nutrients* *nutrition*	*composite meal* *basal metabolic rate* *cholesterol* *folic acid* *polyunsaturated fats* *antioxidants*
Mathematics	8–9 years	Geometry	*angle* *symmetry* *vertical* *horizontal* *triangle* *mirror*	*obtuse* *acute* *isosceles* *equilateral* *quadrant*	*orientation* *reflex* *perpendicular* *trapezium*
Design and Technology	7–9 years	Making a seat	*leg* *seat* *back* *office chair* *dentist chair* *settee* *throne* *shape* *model*	*structure* *function* *individual* *handmade* *mass produced* *prototype* *assemble* *stable* *reinforce*	*linear* *mechanism* *corrugated* *gathered* *eyelet*

Subject	Age group	Topic	Anchor	Goldilocks	Step on
Maths	9–10 years	Measurement	*metric diagrams perimeter units metre litre*	*convert imperial equivalent capacity mass*	*rectilinear equivalences notation*
Science	10–11 years	Forces in action	*still not moving weigh result predict experiment*	*stationary gravity upthrust variables resistance friction forces*	*Newton force meter velocity kinetic Galileo*

Teach

After selecting the vocabulary to be taught, the next part of the STAR sequence is 'teach'. This process has many elements but once both teachers and students become familiar with it, **the 'teach' process should take less than five minutes**. It is essential that the process is kept short as there needs to be daily teaching of words. If too long is spent on the 'teach' process, then there will not be enough time for teaching the variety of words needed.

Words which are sourced from topics will be planned and so there will be opportunity for some preparation such as gathering a symbol and thinking about a child-friendly definition.

In one lesson it is advised to teach one new 'Goldilocks' word to the whole class. This enables the word to be taught to a depth, but the teach sequence is only the beginning of the process. It starts the process that is then built upon during the activate and review phases.

The teach sequence has been developed in response to what is known about how children learn words, and to be accessible for all students. It has been used in a great number of schools internationally now, and proven to be easy to implement, engaging and effective.

The teaching sequence can be presented and adapted according to the words being taught and the context, but the key components should remain the same.

Teach: where to start

- Teach the word quickly using the STAR Topic Word Wizard. Once confident, aim for this process to take five minutes.

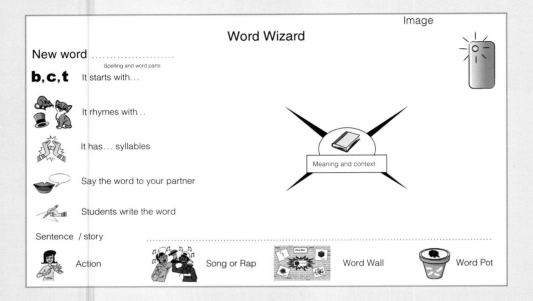

Summary of STAR Topic teaching sequence and rationale for each element

	Component	Rationale
New word: _____ Spelling/word parts	**The word** • Adults write the word on the Word Wizard by 'New word' • Underline any spelling patterns • Draw a line through the word to indicate prefix, base and suffix if applicable e.g.: new word: *settle/ment*	Knowledge of spelling will promote students' writing. Knowledge of morphology contributes to word learning skills and spelling. Research indicates that seeing the written word makes it more likely to be retained.
	Image Use a picture, symbol or drawing that represents the word accompanied by the written word.	Spoken words are fleeting but an image is more permanent. Having both the word and image reduces working memory load.
b, c, t Transparent	**Say and write** • clap syllables • rhyme • initial sound • say to partner • student writes the word	When we are talking it can be hard to clearly identify each word, so this step emphasises the word's phonology (speech sounds) and ensures that the phonology of the word is well-established before the meaning components are added. Builds the bridge for students to use in writing.

	Component	Rationale
	Semantics (meaning) Provide child-friendly definition, context and model how to use the word.	This is the key step. The definition needs to be simple, succinct and provide the key information about the word, that will then be built upon in later steps. Simple language provides basic information. Reduces chances of misunderstanding.
I like the hot and humid **climate** in India.	**Sentence and story** Use the word in a meaningful sentence. Tell a story where you experienced the word (if applicable).	This gives the word a meaningful grammatical context and shows how the word can be used.
	Action Act it out where possible.	An action adds to the meaning, but is also a recall strategy
	Song Sing a song or say a rap.	Children repeat the word, so they are all aware of it, and by saying it are more likely to say it again.
	Word Wall The word and picture go on the Word Wall.	This gives the word a profile, but also builds in opportunities for reviewing the word at a later point.

	Component	Rationale
	Word Pot The word goes into the Word Pot for reviewing in the future.	The Word Pot provides a second review opportunity.

This information can then be summarised on the Word Wizard sheet which can be displayed to the class either electronically or in paper form. Completed copies can be saved for future reference. A blank Word Wizard is available for download from the companion website.

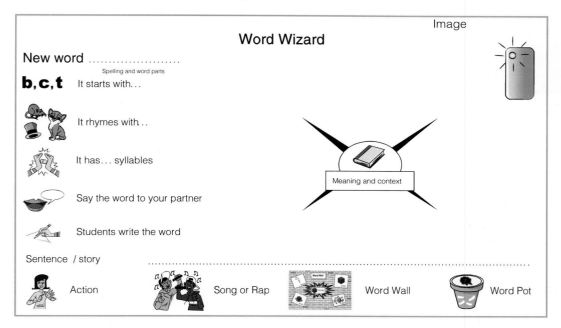

Further detail of STAR Topic teaching sequence

New word

The target word is written on the sheet. Discuss and underline any familiar or unfamiliar spelling patterns as the students will need to be able to use the word in their writing. It is also a time to highlight any prefixes and/or suffixes if applicable. The base word will then become more obvious. Recognising words within a word can aid comprehension. This is simply done by drawing a line between different sections of the word.

filtra~~tion~~	urban~~isa~~~~tion~~
eco~~s~~ystem	spher~~i~~cal
immigra~~tion~~	wat~~er~~proof
signific~~ance~~	nega~~tive~~

Image

In STAR Topic you will have the chance to plan ahead, so find a symbol or image that represents the target word. Present the written word underneath the symbol. Online images can be used, but for more abstract words specific symbol resources such as Communicate in Print (www.widgit.com), Boardmaker (www.mayer-johnson.com), Twinkl Create (www.twinkl.co.uk/create) or ARASAAC (arasaac.org) are often more time efficient. Twinkl create and ARASAAC are both free and more limited compared to the others which are more extensive, but also charge. Finding suitable symbols occasionally requires the use of imaginative search terms.

Say and write

  b, c, t

- Clap syllables: instruct the class to clap out the syllables of the word as they say the word.
- Rhyme: how many rhyming words can the class think of? These can be real or nonsense words. The purpose is that they highlight the speech sounds of the target word.
- Initial sound: what speech sound does the word start with?
- Say the word to a partner: instruct the children to say the word to another child.
- Students write the word: if practical, instruct the children to write the word quickly. It can be on a whiteboard or notebook, but it may be more practical for children to write the new word at another point.

Semantics (meaning)

Before you start teaching you need a clear, succinct, child-friendly definition. It is sometimes quite a challenge to define, even familiar words, precisely, succinctly and simply. It is therefore advised that you look up words in the dictionary. The best online dictionary we have found is www.collinsdictionary.com. For each word in the online dictionary there are different definitions on different tabs, with the first tab providing the most straightforward definition. For instance, the word **evidence** is defined under the first tab as:

'**Evidence** is anything that you see, experience, read, or are told that causes you to believe that something is true or has really happened.'

The 'English' and 'American' tabs provide more complete but complex definitions, for instance for **evidence**:

'ground for belief or disbelief; data on which to base proof or to establish truth or falsehood'.

Even though the first definition is simpler it is still necessary to check that both the vocabulary and grammar are accessible to the children. The word being taught is a 'Goldilocks' word and so it needs to be defined in 'Anchor' words that the children understand. Definitions should only contain words that are easily accessible to the whole class. Sentences should be as simple and short as possible.

The Collins COBUILD range of dictionaries contains similar definitions to the first tab, on the Collins website, with the student versions of the COBUILD range offering simple definitions for a more limited number of words.

In our experience the definition is critical, and so generating a precise but simple definition is worth spending time upon.

With the children, start off by exploring their current understanding of the word by asking them what they know about the word. Children's **relevant** contributions can also be added to a Word Wizard sheet or slide. Irrelevant contributions should be ignored. Add any important information about the word that the children have not mentioned. If the children have very little knowledge or to speed up the process, it may be necessary for the teacher to provide the definition at the start.

The definition that is written on the Word Wizard is not meant to be a full precise dictionary definition. It is meant to give the children enough information to get them going and to add knowledge and understanding as they continue to hear the words in context.

Some of the words have opposites which are commonly taught together e.g. **condensation** and **evaporation**. Particular care needs to be taken with these; see page 155 for further details.

Some words are words that are complex and hard to grasp e.g. **environment, depend, properties** (see 'slippery' words page 174). Take extra care with defining these type of words and providing examples.

Sentence/story

Use a sentence and/or a story to add meaning.

Sentence

> I take **vitamins** every day because they are good for me

As a class, generate a sentence which contains the word. The sentence needs to reflect the meaning of the word. For instance, if the targeted word is **vitamins**, a sentence such as, 'I take **vitamins** every day' does not add any meaning to **vitamins**. A sentence such as, 'I take **vitamins** every day because they are good for me' is more meaningful. It may be necessary to ask for several children's contributions in order to build a meaningful sentence. Encouraging children to use 'because', may be helpful. Summarise the discussion by adding a meaningful sentence to the STAR Topic Word Wizard.

Story for examine

'At my last school there was an outbreak of headlice, so the headteacher wrote to all the parents and asked them to **examine** their children's hair and look very carefully for any headlice. Teachers needed to do it too. **Examining** for headlice takes time, as they are very small. My husband did not put his glasses on when I asked him to **examine** my hair, but he said he could not see any. My head got really itchy so at school I had to ask one of the other teachers to **examine** my hair. She was much better at **examining**, because she looked carefully and closely (and did not need glasses). She found lots and lots of headlice!'

A certain level of dramatic license is permitted, as the aim is for children to be talking about the story and developing an understanding of the word within a context, which can then be referred back to.

A phrase, word or picture can be added to the STAR Topic Word Wizard to remind the children of the story. A quick drawing of a headlice would work in this example!

Action

Act out the word where possible. Be creative. Actions may involve one child, a group or the whole class. They do not need to be formal sign language, such as Makaton. This is appropriate for both younger and older children and as well as being beneficial, it engages a wider group of word learners. An action for 'filtration' could be acting out pouring and filtering liquid; for 'negative' it could be shaking the head and frowning and for 'immigration' it could be flying in an airplane from one house to another.

Song or rap

Sing a song or do a rap. There are songs and a rap available to print from the companion website. The songs are available on YouTube if you search 'Word Aware songs'. The lyrics can be photocopied or printed and used as prompts. The repetition of the target word within these songs helps the children to strengthen their understanding of the word's speech sounds and hence aid memory. Children of all ages respond well to both the songs and the rap. Choose whichever ones you prefer.

WORD SONG

The word for today is X, X, X

The word for today is X

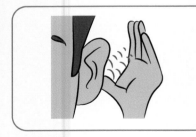

Listen out for X

LEARNING WORDS

WORD RAP

Say the word. . .

Clap the word. . .

Read the word. . .

Act the word. . .

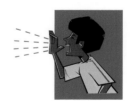

Shout the word. . .

Whisper the word. . .

LEARNING WORDS

 SPELL IT OUT SONG

	Give me a/an …, Give me a/an …, Give me a/an …, What does it spell?
	What did you say?
	Say it again?
	Now clap it out
	And act it out
	And say it one last time

LEARNING WORDS

Word Wall

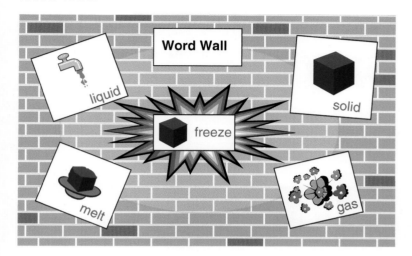

Word Walls start the 'review' segment of the STAR process. Their main purpose is to remind adults and children of the words they are learning, so they are not forgotten. Word Walls can be organised in a way that works for you in your classroom. It is a <u>working</u> Word Wall and so the words go up as they are taught. It should be interactive, so that words that are displayed are all discussed and referred to. Having images as well as words is key to engagement with the Word Wall. New words are placed on the starburst in (see page 208) the middle of the Word Wall. Placing the Word Wall at child height will facilitate them removing the words to assist with their independent writing. Further guidance on creating and interacting with the Word Wall is on page 182.

Word Pot

Another key component of the 'review' part of STAR is the Word Pot. This can be any tub or box where words are easily stored and accessible. A copy of the word and image (or just the written word) are printed or written on a small card and placed in the Word Pot. From time to times random words are selected from the pot and discussed briefly.

The pot can be enhanced by attaching written questions to the outside which the adult can use as prompts when reviewing words. See page 191 for further details of how to make a Word Pot and games to play to review words. Stickers with the prompt questions may also be purchased cheaply from Language for Learning: http://www.languageforlearning.co.uk/shop/Foundation-Stage-and-Key-Stages-1-and-2/Vocabulary

Teach example

This is an example of the STAR Topic teaching sequence for the word **habitats**, taken from the topic of 'Living things and their habitats'.

Symbol

Place a picture or symbol that represents the word such as this one on the Word Wizard.

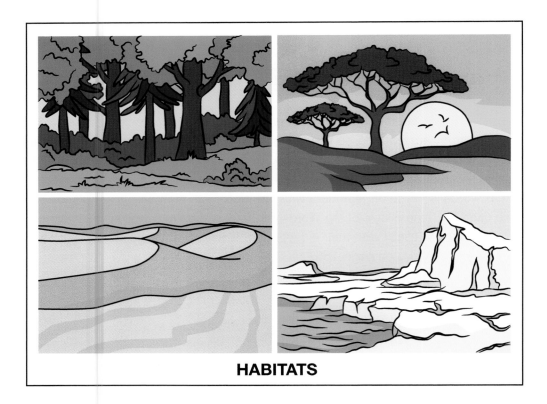

HABITATS

Phonology (speech sounds)

Instruct the class to say the word '**habitats**'. All say the word and clap the syllables together. Ask children to identify what the first sound/phoneme of the word is. Generate real rhyming words or non-words, for example, 'jabitats' or 'sabitats'. Encourage all to say the word '**habitats**' to their friend. All children write the word **habitats** on their mini whiteboards.

Semantics (meaning)

Lead a class discussion about the meaning of the word. Add children's relevant contributions to the Word Wizard. The children may offer very little or use the image and suggest 'forest' or 'desert'. The Collins online dictionary (www.collinsdictionary.com) defines **habitat** as: 'The **habitat** of an animal or plant is the natural environment in which it normally lives or grows.' Key words from this definition should be used, but only if they are anchor words, so best to avoid words like 'natural'

and 'environment' at this point. Add key information in short phrases to the Word Wizard: for example, 'where animals live in the wild'. 'Where you find plants growing in nature.' This is not a full definition at this point as the purpose is to build basic understanding that will be built on by general teaching.

Sentence

As a class generate a meaningful sentence that contains the word. Make sure that the sentence reflects the meaning of the target word.

For example, 'The tree grows in its **habitat**' provides little indication of the meaning of the word **habitat** unless a learner has significant knowledge of the topic.

'The oak tree's **habitat** is a forest' gives more clues to the meaning.

Action

Encourage the class to think up an action. For **habitat** it might be a gesture for 'house' with fingertips held together above the head, to indicate **habitat** is where plants and animals live, or to be more specific a combination of gestures for 'house' and 'animal'.

Song

All the children join in with the rap:
'Say the word **habitat**.'
'Clap the word **habitat**.' (three claps)
'Read the word **habitat**.' (adult points to the word on the whiteboard)
'Act the word': all do the action '**habitat**', as described above.
'Shout the word **habitat**!'
'Whisper the word **habitat**.'

Word Wall

The word and symbol for **habitat** is put onto the Word Wall by a child.

Word Pot

The word is written on a small card and placed in the Word Pot.

Word Wizard

New word *habitat* ....

b, c, t   It starts with   *h*
Spelling and word parts

It rhymes with... *habitat*

It has... **3** ... syllables

Say the word to your partner

Students write the word

Sentence / story ....   *In a forest habitat there are lots of trees, and deer, but also insects*

Action

Image

Plants grow
in nature

Animals live in
habitats in the wild

Meaning and context

Living things

Forests and deserts

Word Wall

Word Pot

Song or Rap

Activate

After 'select' and 'teach' the next step in the STAR process is 'activate'. Activate is a vital stage in which the children are given the opportunity to explore the meaning of the word in relation to their own knowledge. By linking the new word to practical activities children gain a deeper understanding of it.

Activating a word can be done as part of any lesson as the Goldilocks word that has been selected from that topic will directly link to what is being taught. As with a regular lesson the subject that the word relates to is explored with a variety of practical activities and discussion. To fully activate a word a few additions are required.

- Start with an expectation that children should use the word. e.g.: 'Today I am going to listen out for use of the word **data**.'

- Praise when the word is used.

- Prompt when opportunities arise when it could have been used, e.g.: 'Tell me about that again, using the word **attributes**.'

- Encourage sentence responses including the word.

- Ask questions that require application, such as talking through experiments or practical exercises or applying the word in a new way.

Activate: where to start

- Ensure the word is visible on the Word Wall and highlight this to the children.

- Continue to use simple terms to define the words, as well as simple synonyms. If not direct synonyms, then explain the differences.

- Model use of the target word in different contexts as much as possible so that the children hear it many times and learn more about the word from hearing its natural use.

- Continue to give examples of how the word relates to the children's lives as well as the topic being studied.

- Clarify potential misunderstandings.

- Encourage students to use the new word. Provide feedback on their efforts, e.g.: 'In science today I am going to be listening out for children using our new scientific vocabulary which is there on our Word Wall' or 'When talking about the foods we eat challenge yourself to use the word **nutrition**.'

Activate: example

Habitat is taught as part of a science lesson exploring living things and their habitats. **Habitat** will be encountered naturally in this lesson. To activate the word, it is prominently displayed on the Word Wall and adults use it where they can, emphasising the word when they do use it. Children are encouraged to use the word verbally as well as to remove the word from the Word Wall to assist with any writing. For instance, **habitat** will be used many times in a lesson in which child explore and compare natural **habitats**.

Activation for words which are more complex and harder to grasp

The general aim of the 'activate' phase is for children to independently take their understanding of the word and develop this within their own understanding of the world. Doing this works well once children have a threshold of knowledge of the new word but can be problematic when they do not understand enough about the word. Words which represent new concepts, particularly if they are abstract, generally take a bit longer to develop full understanding.

These words are often hard for children to grasp and so we have coined the term 'slippery' words. The teach process is the same as other words but because the words are harder to grasp extra guidance is needed during the 'activate' stage so that children are able to deepen their understanding before going on to fully independent activation as described in 'Activate: where to start' (see page 210).

Examples of 'slippery' words

environment, depend, properties, volume, friction, disperse, relationship, data, probable, range, attribute, reasonable, ecosystem, evaporation, amplitude criteria, globalisation, ratio, economy, consistency, evidence, particles, variables, mass, food chain, obtuse, quadrant

'Slippery' words should be identified at the planning stage. The selected Goldilocks words should be analysed to identify words which may require further activation. Sometimes words may appear to be complex and hard to grasp but if a simple but complete definition is provided then the children are able to understand it. These words should still be treated with caution, and great care taken with the definition and examples.

Example of complex words which appear to be 'slippery' words but can be defined with simple words so do not need additional activate activities

Complex word	Simple definition
population density	The number of people who live in an area
transparent	See through
significance	How important something is

On other occasions, even experienced practitioners may be surprised when during teaching it becomes apparent that the new word is proving to be challenging for children and it requires further activation.

Sometimes words appear quite straightforward, but children have difficulty understanding them because they confuse the new words with other terms. Opposites or words which are closely related such as **orbit** and **rotation** or **area** and **perimeter** should not be introduced at the same time. See page 155.

'Slippery' words are usually abstract, and so the trap is that we explain these complicated words with lots of further complicated words, which of course many students are not be able to access. The challenge is therefore to convey abstract meaning via simple, precise language and multisensory learning, so think hard about what hands on opportunities can be provided, and simple language that can be used.

'Slippery' words do take longer to embed, but time spent on the initial phase will ensure deeper understanding and less time spent later on clarifying errors. Do not try teaching 'slippery' words quickly, as that may sow the seeds of future confusion.

'Slippery' words activation process

Use a combination of:

1. Hands-on learning
2. If hands-on learning is not possible then provide infographics or short videos
3. Provide accessible examples
4. Support connections to what children already know
5. Support children to use the new term

Simple language used at each step

1. Hands-on learning

The best way of understanding a complex 'slippery' word is via hands-on learning accompanied by simple language. This gives children the opportunity to develop an understanding of the new word and its context with very little language.

Where possible start with hands-on learning. There are two types of hands-on learning:

- 'Body' refers to activities in which students experience the new word without any equipment or objects.
- 'Object' is about experiencing the word with objects.

Try and do both where you can.

From our list of examples of 'slippery' words, some are easier to do hands-on learning with than others:

Possible to do hands-on learning (either/or 'body' and 'object')	Harder to do hands-on learning
Depend, properties, friction, consecutive, approximately, disperse, data, evaporation, condensation, evidence, variables, horizontal, amplitude, probable, volume, attribute, criteria, ratio, consistency, relationship, range, reasonable, economy, particles	**Ecosystem, globalisation, environment**

Hands-on learning examples

Body	Use just your body to experience the word. Objects are not used.	<ul><li>Feeling **friction** by rubbing hands together</li><li>A group of children **disperse** around the room.</li><li>Holding up another child so they **depend** on you.</li><li>Doing a Mexican wave in **consecutive** order.</li><li>Walking around the **perimeter** of the playground.</li><li>Measure the height of everyone. Then put all the **data** into a table. An object, the tape measure, is being used but it is in relation to children's bodies.</li><li>Choose children by different **criteria** e.g. male, over x height, wearing a jumper.</li><li>Holding your arm **horizontal.**</li><li>Before you start a race between the teacher and the fastest runner in the class, think about the **probable** winner.</li><li>Ask, 'I am going to guess that we have 45 people in this room. Is that a **reasonable** guess?'</li></ul>
Object	Using objects to help understand the word. This could be a practical experiment or just a quick experience.	<ul><li>Experimenting with the different **properties** of paperclips, plastic forks, straws and rubber bands.</li><li>Measuring the **volume** of a cup using water and a measuring jug.</li><li>Work out **approximately** how many stones there are in a pile.</li><li>Put ink in water and watch how it **disperses**. Blowing a dandelion seed head and watch how it **disperses.**</li><li>Do an experiment where you predict the **probable** outcome.</li><li>Trial making different **consistencies** with water and flour.</li><li>Making different **amplitudes** of waves using rope and Slinkys.</li><li>Role-playing buying, selling and saving to illustrate the **economy**.</li><li>Put balls in a box to demonstrate **particles**.</li></ul>

2. If hands-on learning is not possible then provide infographics or short videos

Hands-on learning provides a richer multi-sensory experience so it is preferred, but if it is not possible then infographics or short videos that focus specifically on the word's meaning should be used.

Specifically explain how the image relates to the word, as it may not be clear to children who do not know the word. Only use videos or excerpts that focus on the meaning of one word at this point as more general videos may be too complex and result in confusion.

Particles

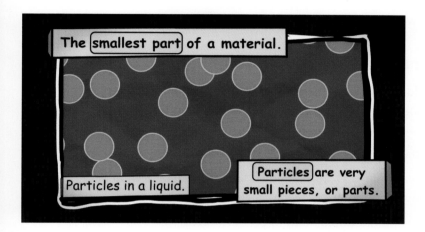

The authors have worked with Lift lessons, who have produced a series of videos which give clear and simple definitions of science-related terminology such as the example above for 'particles'. (See www. liftlessons.co)

For **ecosystem** images of tropical rainforest **ecosystems**, woodland **ecosystems** and desert **ecosystems** should be displayed and discussed using simple language.

Ecosystem

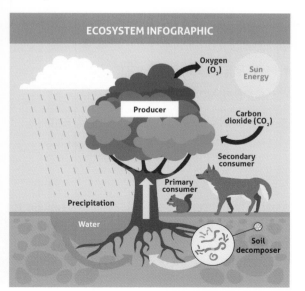

Economy

3. Provide accessible examples

Explicitly link the knowledge that children are developing to other familiar contexts. Provide examples of the word that children can relate to. The language used should continue to be simple, with Anchor words that children are familiar with and short sentences and avoid using any new terms which may be confused with the target word.

For example, for **friction**: 'When we rubbed our hands together it got warm because of **friction**. Friction happens at other times too. If you slide on the carpet, it quickly gets hot because of **friction**. When you are on a skateboard on a flat road you have to keep pushing off. If you don't, you will slow down because of **friction** between the wheels and the ground.'

4. Support connections to what the children already know

Using prompt questions, encourage children to make their own links back to terms and contexts with which they are already familiar. This embeds the new word into their own understanding.

Connect to familiar situations	• What things do we use for gym that are **horizontal**? • If you asked your mum/dad/carer if you could stay out late, what is the **probable** answer? • What **data** do weather people need to collect? • What are the **attributes** of an umbrella? • How long will it take to get things to boil in the pan? This will take different amounts of time depending on what? What are the **variables**? • What can you say about the **environment** that we live in? Think about things like the amount of grass, trees, buildings, type of weather. • Let's name lots of different things in the woodland **ecosystem**. Think of the wood behind our school.
This word is a bit like . . .? How is it different from that word	• **Approximately** is a bit like **guess**. How is it different? • **Disperse** is a bit like **spread out**. How is it different? • **Ratio** is a bit like **compare**. How is it different? This requires sophisticated language skills and some students will need some support.

5. Support children to use the new term

By this step, children will have heard the new word and how to use it numerous times. This will have helped to embed the word in their understanding and so the next stage is to extend this, so they start using the word.

- Start with an expectation that children should use the word. e.g.: 'Today I am going to listen out for use of the word **data**.'
- Praise when the word is used.
- Prompt when opportunities arise when it could have been used. e.g.: 'Tell me about that again, using the word **attributes**.'

- Encourage sentence responses including the word.
- Ask more connect questions (as in point 4 'Support connections to what the children already know' above) but this time expect complete sentences including the target word.

Review

The final part of the STAR process for teaching words is 'review'.

'My students don't retain the words that they've been taught!' is a common complaint of many a teacher. The two most likely causes of this are that the word has not been taught to enough depth to start with or that the children have not encountered the word enough at later times. The 'teach' and 'activate' elements above will deal with teaching the word to depth, and so our attention now moves to 'review'. Reviewing words provides students with further opportunities to assimilate words into their vocabularies as well as ensuring that they are not forgotten.

As there is no spare time in the school day, the challenge is to find review activities which are either very quick or which children do spontaneously and independently. Review activities which involve students reflecting on the words' meanings will be far more beneficial than word searches, copying or spelling which only engage superficial knowledge. Establish a few good habits from the outset and reviewing words will become second nature.

Review: where to start

- Review the word at the end of the lesson
- Play a Word Wall clue game with all of the words once a week e.g. Fly swat game (see page 183)
- Take ten words out of the Word Pot each week and talk about them (see page 191). This can be spread out over the week.

Review the word at the end of the lesson

Talk about the word again and review what has been learnt by asking a few questions along the lines of: 'What was the word we learnt today again?', 'During the lesson, what did you learn about the word?', 'Let's all clap the word together' and 'Let's act the word together'. Encourage students to take responsibility for their word learning by asking them, 'When do you think you might use this word again?' and 'Tell the person next to you how you will remember the word.'

Notice and use the word at other times

The 'Goldilocks' words have been selected from one particular topic, but many will have applications outside of the original topic. Be aware of the words that have been taught and if you encounter them in other contexts then highlight them to the class. Also try and use the words in the coming weeks. With everything else to remember it can be a challenge, but the words will be on the Word Wall to remind you.

Listen out for the word tally

Choose three words that you have already taught. Write the words on a tally chart (see next page) and display it prominently. Prompt children to listen out and look out for the words. They can add a tally when they identify the word whenever it is used. When used in the classroom, they just put their hand up if they hear the word or show an adult when they encounter it in reading. Outside of the classroom they need to remember the sentence and context the word was in. Fictional examples are acceptable so long as an appropriate context is offered. When children use one of the words in their writing then this also gets a point. The points are tallied collectively, as a class. (Based on the work of Beck et al., 2002)

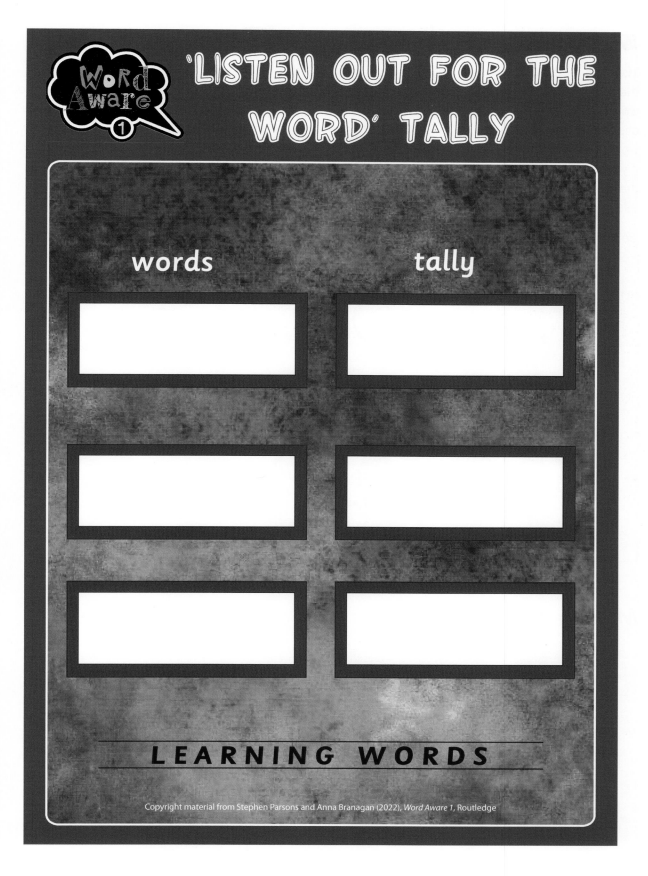

Word Mats

Make Word Mats for each subject. These are then placed on each table with words and images for all the 'Goldilocks' words in that topic. These are then colour coded by subject so the children can find the words easily. The school should agree on a colour coding system. It does not matter which colours you choose, just make sure it is consistent, e.g.: science is red, geography is green. If you are teaching one word a day, you will not be able to specifically teach every 'Goldilocks' word for every subject. However, if you do have a picture to go with each of the key words this will help children assimilate knowledge through normal teaching and start to use the key words in their writing. Our late friend Pip St. John used this approach to great effect (St. John & Vance, 2014).

Below is a Word Mat example for all the 'Goldilocks' words for a geography topic.

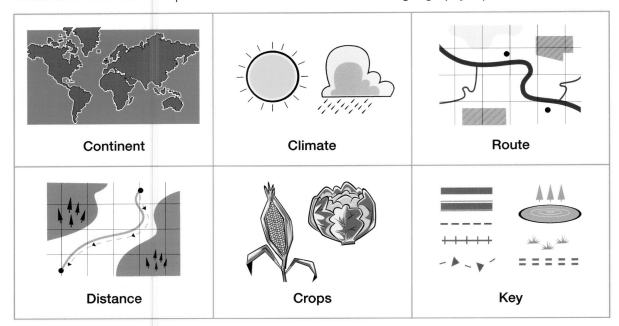

Making a Word Wall

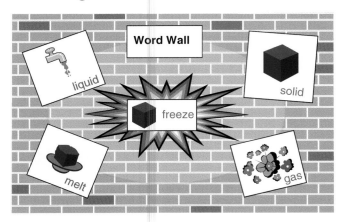

A Word Wall is a place to display words that have been introduced. This is a key strategy to reinforce vocabulary as it gives words a high profile in the classroom and can also be used as a prompt. The Word

Wall can be organised in a manner that works for you. It might be that you have one section for topic and another for literacy words. We have seen great Word Walls on pillars and on cupboard doors.

Key points:

- It is a <u>working</u> Word Wall and so the words should be added to the wall as part of the lesson in which they are introduced.

- Words from STAR Topic should be accompanied by a relevant symbol or clear image. These may be quick drawings.

- The latest word should be highlighted by placing it on a starburst. An example of a starburst is provided on page 208.

- The words should be kept at child height so that they can be pulled off and used in the children's writing.

- Words should be interacted with at different points in the day and in different ways. Below are a number of ideas.

Word Wall games

Reviewing words that are on the Word Wall will bring them to life and ensure that they do not become forgotten 'wallpaper'. Many of these games can be used with words from other sources as well, such as the Word Pot. And of course, feel free to play your own games, as long as they require students to think about the words' meanings. Get into the habit of playing these regularly for a few minutes. Build up a repertoire of class favourites.

Word Wall definition clues

A student or adult gives a clue about a word from the Word Wall. Others try to guess what the word is. To support students to give better clues use the structure outlined below. See page 185 for a printable version, which can also be downloaded from the companion website.

- This word is a bit like . . . but . . .

- This word can be used when talking about . . . especially when . . .

- This word is particularly useful because . . .

- I would use this word when I am talking about . . .

- A special thing about this word is . . .

- The thing that will help me remember this word is . . .

Variations:

- **Fly swat** Two children are given a plastic fly swat each. They stand either side of the Word Wall. A third player gives a clue and the children hit the target word. The child then states what the target was.

- **It's behind you** Child stands in front of the Word Wall with their back to it and an adult or another child describes a word (without using the word directly). The child must identify the target word.

Stand up if you have

Each child writes a word or is given a word from the Word Wall. Without naming the word the teacher defines or gives clues about one word from the Word Wall. Children stand up once they think the teacher is talking about their word. The first child to respond successfully becomes the next one to define/give clues.

Pictograms

Select words from the Word Wall and write them in a shape which conveys meaning. Objects with distinctive shapes are most successful, for instance, 'thermometer', 'hurricane', 'magnet', 'growth' or 'orbit'.

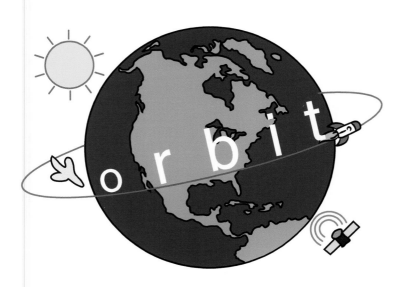

Word Wall Definition Clues

This word is a kind of . . .	The thing that will help me remember this word is . . .
This word is particularly useful because . . .	This word is someone who can . . .
This word is something that can . . .	This word is something that . . . . can do when . . .
This word is used . . .	This word is like . . . but . . .
Something that is described by this word is . . .	Someone who is described by this word is . . .

R E V I E W I N G   W O R D S

Say it in a sentence

In pairs or small groups ask the children to use a target word in a sentence, for example, 'Make up a sentence with the word **carbohydrate** in it?' Response could be: 'My favourite **carbohydrate** is chips.' Each group then shares their sentence verbally or writes it on the board.

Collecting class knowledge

Each student takes one word and interviews three others about the word. They then integrate this together and add their own knowledge to come up with a 'perfect' definition. These can be recorded and shared.

Connections

Select two words from the Word Wall that are related in some way. It may be a direct or indirect connection. Ask several children to explain how the two maybe connected, as there may be multiple ways for them to be connected. Encourage sentence responses. Answers may be written down.

Word Wall review cards

Give each child a square of card or use the version on the next page. Each student selects a word from the Word Wall and writes it at the top of the card. They then write three things about the word. Provide structure as per the Word Wall definition clues if required.

When complete, mix the class set together and then read them one at a time, encouraging the children to guess. If some clues are not successful talk about how they could be improved. The cards may be kept after the Word Wall words have been changed and used as a long-term review activity. These can be downloaded from the companion website.

Word Wall review cards

Word _____	Word _____
Three things about the word: 　1. 　2. 　3.	**Three things about the word:** 　1. 　2. 　3.
Word _____	Word _____
Three things about the word: 　1. 　2. 　3.	**Three things about the word:** 　1. 　2. 　3.
Word _____	Word _____
Three things about the word: 　1. 　2. 　3.	**Three things about the word:** 　1. 　2. 　3.

Reverse review cards

Students write the word on one side of a card and its definition on the other. Students move around the class holding the word outwards and the definition faced towards themselves. When two students meet, they take in turns defining each other's words and check what is said against the definition on the card. When completed they swap words and move about to talk to other students.

Word spinner

Using the spinner pictured below. Fix a plastic spinner in the middle of the circle. Some classes have attached the spinner next to the Word Wall as a way of making it more interactive. Select a word from the Word Wall. The children take turns to spin and carry out the relevant instruction about the target word.

These free online spinners may be edited to create word challenges. Create an account and create a spinner at:

- wheeldecide.com

- wheelofnames.com

- classtools.net/random-name-picker

Add to the fun and complexity by adding a second spinner (you may need to open the second online spinner in a separate window) with one containing word challenges and the other the target words:

Spinner 1: word challenges

1. Say the first sound
2. Act out the word
3. Use the word in a sentence
4. Clap the syllables
5. Say one thing about the word's meaning
6. When might you next use the word?
7. How will you remember the word?

Spinner 2:

Six words from the Word Wall or Word Pot.

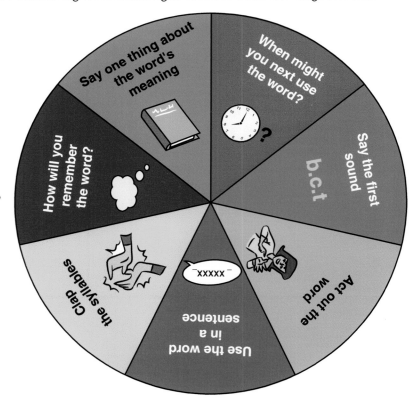

Definition match

Select words from the Word Wall. Write words and their definitions on separate cards, and then mix them up. Some children are given the words and some are given definitions. They then move around the room matching the words with their definitions.

An example is below:

Melt	To change from a solid into a liquid as a result of being heated up.
Freeze	To change from a liquid to a solid by the reduction of temperature, such as water to ice.
Evaporate	To change from a liquid to a gas.
Condensing	To change from a gas to a liquid.

(Based on the work of Beck et al., 2002.)

Topic connections

Give each group of children the same six or more Word Wall words written on pieces of card. Ask the children to arrange the cards according to how the words are connected, so that closely connected words are adjacent and less related words further apart. Encourage discussion. Children may then move around the class to look at other groups' arrangements and ask questions about how they came to their decisions.

Reflections on word learning

Students copy six of the words from the Word Wall onto the following table. They then rate their own level of knowledge of the word. Students then pick two words they wish to consolidate.

Reflections on Word Learning

Name: .... Date: ....

Topic/s: ....

Copy six words from the Word Wall. Then rate your knowledge and skills, and then choose two words to learn more about

Word from the Word Wall	How well I can say what it means			How well I can say it in a sentence			Tick the words I have chosen to learn even more about
	😃	😐	🙁	😃	😐	🙁	☐
							☐
							☐
							☐
							☐
							☐

How I will learn more about the two words I have chosen

REVIEWING WORDS

Long term Word Wall review games

The words will remain on the Word Wall for the length of the topic, which may only be about six weeks or so. Long-term review is also necessary. Although the curriculum moves from one topic to the next, it is still important to come back and revisit words from previous topics.

Take a photo

Take a photo of the Word Wall and project it onto the whiteboard once in a while and play any of the games listed above.

Word Wall book

Make the photo of the Word Wall the cover of your topic book. Within the book devote a page to each word. Children illustrate a page which shows each word's meaning. If kept in the book corner students may occasionally select the book and review words independently.

Reviewing words with the Word Pot

Word Pots are an effective way to review words that have been taught in class using the STAR approach. It works in conjunction with the Word Wall, as words may be kept in the Word Pot for a lengthier time period.

Once the word has been taught, ask a child to write it on a piece of card and add it to your Word Pot. When you have a moment select the word and discuss it with the class (prompt questions are provided below) or play one of the word games.

How to make a Word Pot

Find a container with a lid. It can be any shape so long as it is sturdy and can be closed. Cover it in any attractive paper. Cut out the *Word Aware* symbol to go on the top of the pot. Cut out the question prompts and stick them to the sides of the pot. Both the *Word Aware* symbol and the question prompts are below and on the companion website. They may also be purchased in sticker format from www. languageforlearning.co.uk.

https://www.languageforlearning.co.uk/shop/Foundation-Stage-and-Key-Stages-1-and-2/Vocabulary

What can it do?	What does it look like?	Describe it to your friend.
Can you think of something that can be described as (target word)?	What verb does it describe or go with?	When might someone do this? When might you do this?
Where might you see this word?	Think of a time when you could use this word.	I like/don't like this word because . . .
Which other word is a bit like this word? How is it different from that word?	The author chose this word. What other word could they have used?	How will you remember the word?

Connect 2

Select 10–20 words from the Word Pot. Write them in two columns on the board. An example is provided below. Ask the children to think of connections between words from each list. The task may be completed individually or in small groups and either verbally or written.

rumour	coin
joyfully	settlers
hurtled	hollow
excavate	inky
unison	shiver
radius	aquamarine
reef	frantic
magnify	stagger

Connections could be: **hurtled** and **stagger** as they both describe types of movement; **unison** and **settlers** as **settlers** needed to work together or in **unison** to survive; **reef** and **aquamarine** as a **reef** might be located in beautiful **aquamarine** waters; **radius** and **coin** as we can measure the **radius** of a **coin**. (This game is inspired by Graves, 2009.)

As quick as you can

One child takes a word from the Word Pot. The challenge is for that child to describe the word without using the target word at all so that others are able to guess the word. Another child then becomes the 'caller'.

Against the clock

Similar to 'As quick as you can' but the adult is the caller. The adult takes 10 cards from the Word Pot and places them face down. Set a stopwatch. The caller takes each card in turn and defines the word without using it. Students must not interrupt until the caller nods to indicate she has completed the definition clue. If the caller is interrupted that word is discarded and a new one is added. Try and beat the class record each time you play.

Mini bingo

Take ten to 15 words from the Word Pot and write them on the board. Children write down any three words on a piece of paper. The adult defines words randomly, and students guess the word. They then tick off the word if they have it written down. The first child to tick off their three words calls out 'mini-bingo'. It is then their turn to come to the front and take over the role of defining words for others to guess. As other children call 'mini-bingo' they come to the front to define words. Continue until all words have been defined.

Shaboo

A combination of charades, Taboo and Pictionary that is a fun way to review words.

Before playing:

- Divide the class in two: 'Team A' and 'Team B'.
- Print five copies of the Shaboo cards (on the next page) on to card. Cut out the cards and place them all in one pot (instructions pot).
- Find a dice and the Word Pot (containing words you have previously taught).

Start playing

- A player from 'Team A' player takes a card from the 'instructions' pot and one from the Word Pot. Without showing the word to others they follow the instructions on the card.
- Once the word has been guessed by their team or they have successfully used the word, the player rolls the dice and this number is added to their team's score. That is unless they get the 'lose all points' card!

Adapted from: http://hubpages.com/education/Fun-Game-to-Learn-and-Practice-High-Level-or-ESL-Vocabulary-Words

Shaboo cards

Act It

Read the word on the card silently. Act out the meaning of the word. No noises or air spelling of word is allowed.

Don't Say It

Read the word on the card silently. Without saying the word on the card, define the word to help others guess the correct word.

Draw It

Read the word on the card silently. Draw a picture on the board that shows the meaning of the word. No speaking, gesturing or writing letters.

Use It

This time you can say the word. Use the word in a sentence showing that you understand the meaning.

Synonym

Without saying the word on the card, say 'a synonym of the word on the card is ...' If they do not guess, then add 'this word is a bit like that other word but...'

Something Special

Without saying the word on the card, say something special or unique about it. It might be its spelling, what it means, when it can be used or why you like. Think hard about why it is special.

Take another card and earn double points when you roll the dice

Lose all points. Do not take another card.

Quick quiz

Give four children a different buzzer each or failing that a simple musical instrument or shaker. The caller takes a word from the word pot and continues to give clues until it is guessed. The first player who buzzes in with the correct word is awarded one point. A second point is awarded if the guessing player is also able to use the word in a sentence. The sentence must not be too similar to the clues provided. The player who answers successfully becomes the caller and passes his buzzer to another child.

Creative review games

The activities provided below all require the children to reflect on the words' meanings as they make them. They are also designed so that curious children will pick them up spontaneously and play with from time to time, thus reviewing words as they do so.

One-word book

Create a one-page book by cutting a piece of A4 paper in half then folding each piece in half. On the front page of the 'book' write a word and draw a relevant picture. Inside the book write information about the word including definitions and sentences containing the word. The children's books can then be collected to form a class topic library.

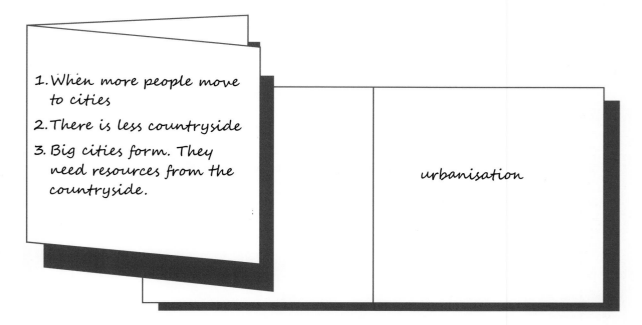

1. When more people move to cities
2. There is less countryside
3. Big cities form. They need resources from the countryside.

urbanisation

Topic dictionary

Students complete either the 'Word Summary' or the 'Reflections on Word Learning' independently (see page 196 and 197). This could also be a homework task. These sheets should be collated and kept for long term review.

Topic word video dictionary

Individual children or groups of children make short videos showing the meaning of the word together with a quick definition. Sometimes moving images have more impact than explanations. The videos can then be collated into a 'dictionary' which can be used for revision, and potentially across the school in future years.

Word Summary

Name: .... Date: ....

Word: .... Topic: ....

| Say it out loud. Tick when you have done it ☐ | Spell it out loud. Tick when you have done it ☐ |

| Write three important things about the word's meaning

 1.

 2.

 3. | Draw a picture showing the word's meaning |

Write a sentence using the word. Make sure your sentence shows that you understand what the word means.

REVIEWING WORDS

Reflections on Word Learning

Name: .... Date: ....

Topic/s: ....

Write the word in the cloud. Then add as much
information as you can about the word on each of the 'spokes'.

REVIEWING WORDS

True or false folding books

Copy and cut out the blank 'True or False Folding Books' from the next page or print from the companion website which accompanies this book. Details of how to access are on page i. Children select words from the Word Wall or the Word Pot and make their own. They then fold them up and write the word on the front cover. Then they ask their peers the questions, e.g. 'True or false: Vitamins are good for you?'

True or false: Vitamins are good for you	☑ True ☐ False	True or false: You can only get vitamins from pills.	☐ True ☒ False	True or false: Fruit has losts of vitamins.	☑ True ☐ False

True or false:

☐ True
☐ False

True or false:

☐ True
☐ False

True or false:

☐ True
☐ False

True or false:

☐ True
☐ False

True or false:

☐ True
☐ False

True or false:

☐ True
☐ False

True or false:

☐ True
☐ False

True or false:

☐ True
☐ False

True or false:

☐ True
☐ False

Vocabulator

Three-quarters fill a large, transparent plastic jar or juice bottle with rice, couscous, pasta or similar. Print words, related to a topic including verbs or adjectives, on small pieces of card and add these to the jar. You may need to attach a key ring or paper clip to each piece of card, to prevent the cards sticking together. Glue or tape the lid shut. The children can then shake or rotate the jar and look for the words. An option is for the children to write down the words they find. Challenges can be added. These are written on pieces of small card which are hole punched in the corner. A ribbon or elastic band is then used to fix to the neck of the bottle. Here is an example of challenges for a geography topic:

Target words: region, location, significance, country, environment, hemisphere, climate, global

Challenges:

- Find a word beginning with 's'.

- Find a word that is something to do with weather.

- UK, Ireland, Finland, Iran and Poland are types of what? Can you find the word?

- Find a word that means 'really important'.

- Which word is a bit like 'place'?

- 'Hemi' means half. Can you find a word with 'hemi' in it?

Inspired by Melissa Forney.

For further inspiration go to: https://www.pinterest.co.uk/wordaware/vocabulary-reviewing-words/

Fortune teller

Make up the fortune teller as instructed below. Select four words from the Word Wall. Write these on the four outside squares of the fortune teller. To play: a player chooses a word. The 'fortune teller' spells out the word in time to the movement of the fortune teller. When the word has been spelt four numbers will be displayed. The player selects one of these. The fortune teller is again moved in time to the numbers being counted. Once the counting is completed a further number is selected. The corresponding flap is lifted, and the question is read out.

How to make a fortune teller

To make a fortune teller follow these instructions:

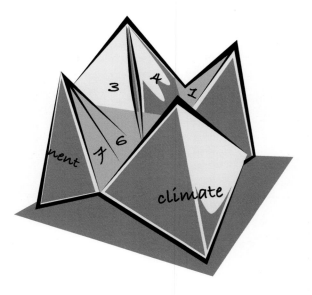

1. Copy and cut out the square design on the next page. Select four words that you wish to review and write one in each of the four blank corners.

2. Fold into quarters, dividing the paper into squares. Then unfold.

3. Place it **face down** and then fold the corners into the centre. You will now have a smaller square.

4. Fold the small square in quarters again so that now you have a very small square.

5. Unfold so that you have the small square back again. Flip it over so the unfolded side is uppermost.

6. Fold the corners into the centre, again creating a very small square.

7. Fold into quarters again so that you now have a tiny square.

8. Unfold once. Place your fingers under the flaps. Hey presto!

Search online for 'How to make a fortune teller' for video demonstrations.

Fortune teller

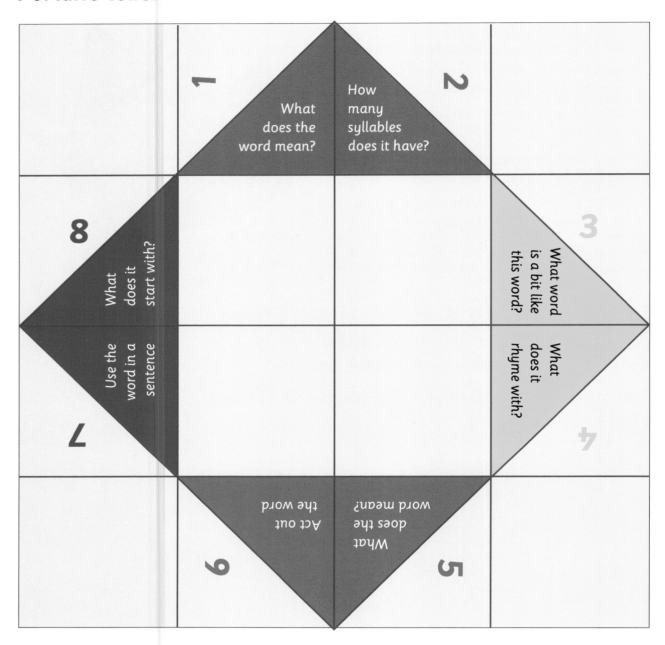

Magic book

Magic books have proved to be one of the big hits on our training courses. They are a fun way that children will spontaneously come back and look at, thus reviewing the words they have been taught.

Make a magic book following the instructions on the next page. Select your vocabulary and definitions prior to commencing the craft element or the words may get lost in the fun! The instructions look complicated, but the books are actually very straightforward and quick to make.

Inspired by Melissa Forney. Also search YouTube for 'vocabulary foldable Martha Estorga' or 'cool vocabulary tools-foldables' for a video demonstration.

How to make a magic book

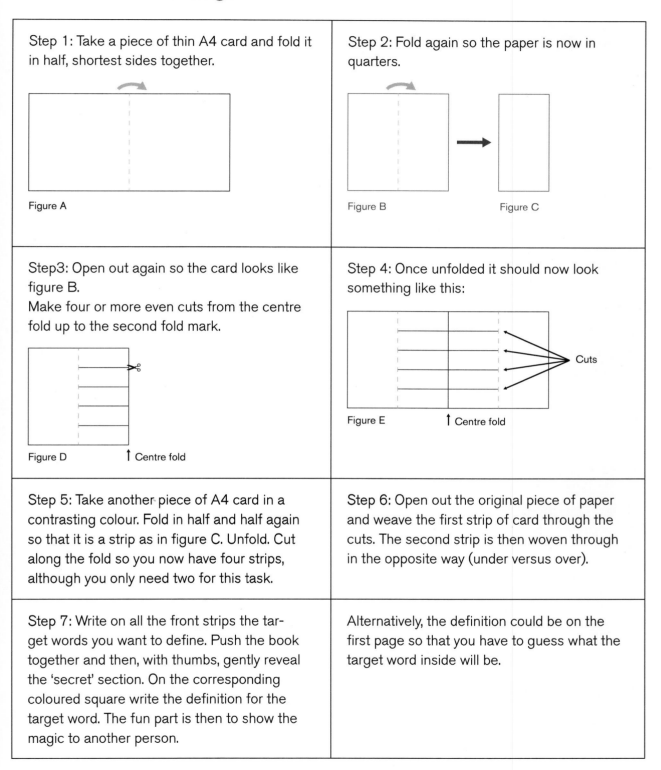

Step 1: Take a piece of thin A4 card and fold it in half, shortest sides together.

Figure A

Step 2: Fold again so the paper is now in quarters.

Figure B   Figure C

Step3: Open out again so the card looks like figure B.
Make four or more even cuts from the centre fold up to the second fold mark.

Figure D   ↑ Centre fold

Step 4: Once unfolded it should now look something like this:

Cuts

Figure E   ↑ Centre fold

Step 5: Take another piece of A4 card in a contrasting colour. Fold in half and half again so that it is a strip as in figure C. Unfold. Cut along the fold so you now have four strips, although you only need two for this task.

Step 6: Open out the original piece of paper and weave the first strip of card through the cuts. The second strip is then woven through in the opposite way (under versus over).

Step 7: Write on all the front strips the target words you want to define. Push the book together and then, with thumbs, gently reveal the 'secret' section. On the corresponding coloured square write the definition for the target word. The fun part is then to show the magic to another person.

Alternatively, the definition could be on the first page so that you have to guess what the target word inside will be.

Homework

Homework will give children the opportunity to be exposed to the target words again and, as it is in a different context, the meaning of each word will be extended. Useful activities include:

- Sending the words home for children to stick on their fridge. Encourage families to use the words in context, so talk about the words rather than ask 'What does that mean?' Use the 'Fridge Words' sheet on page 209 to send home to families.
- Print the word onto sticky labels and give one to each child. Write on the sticker: 'Talk to me about (the word)' and add a symbol if you can.
- Context challenge. Children are challenged to find the word in another context. It may be spoken or written, but it should not be a dictionary. They report back the sentence and the context.
- Word Expert: at home children ask others about the word. If family members are unsure what the word means, they can look it up in an online dictionary. The purpose is for families to talk about words and what they mean.

Examples of a sticker for homework

Talk to me about
the word
continent

Refer to the section below on 'Families' for other ways in which homework can be used to support vocabulary learning.

Review example

The word **habitat** is reviewed at the end of the lesson. The teacher asks, 'Who can think of a sentence using the word **habitat**?'

At the end of the lesson everyone gets a sticker with the word on it. Children are encouraged to go home and talk to their families about the word **habitat.**

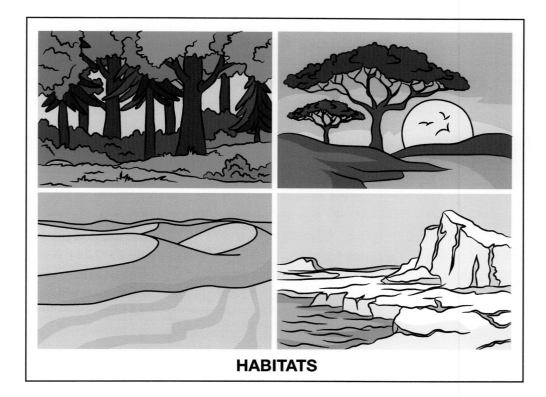

HABITATS

A week later, the topic 'Living things and their habitats' is continued. At the beginning of the lesson the teacher refers back to the word from last week. The class claps the word **habitat** and a child is asked to find it on the Word Wall.

The word is reviewed when the class plays Word Wall definition clues. It also comes out of the pot a week or so later when words are taken from the Word Pot.

How many words to teach?

When starting to use Word Aware begin with teaching **two words per week**. These could be either STAR Topic words or STAR Literacy or one of each. Once confident with the process, then build up to teaching a word a day (**five words per week**).

STAR Topic Planning Sheet

Year group:	Subject:	Topic:
Anchor words	**Goldilocks words** Not too easy and not too hard, but just right	**Step on words**
Children have a thorough understanding of these words. Everyday spoken and written language for a child of this age. Used at home and in daily interactions. Children may have become familiar with this vocabulary through prior teaching.	**Really useful words** Likely to be encountered again in reading or oral language. Average adult has a **good** level of knowledge of the word. Words that are very topic-specific but are core to the topic. Age 7+: Desirable for children to use in their writing.	Less likely to be encountered again in reading or oral language. Average adult does **not have much** knowledge of the word. Words that are particularly topic-specific and are not core to the topic. Age 7+: Not a word that children usually need to use in their own writing.

Image

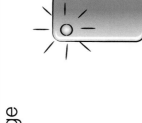

Word Wizard

New word . . . .
Spelling and word parts

b, c, t It starts with. . .

It rhymes with. . .

Meaning and context

It has. . . syllables

Say the word to your partner

Students write the word

Sentence / story

Action

Song or Rap

Word Wall

Word Pot

Today's word is:

Fridge Words

Your child has been learning these new words in school. Please put this sheet on your fridge to remind your child which words they have been learning. Talk to them about the words. Talk about the words rather than ask too many questions. Show your child how you use the words. Take turns with your child to use these words in sentences.

Please stick this on your fridge

Word	Definition

R E V I E W I N G   W O R D S

2.1 Teach Words
STAR Topic: Where to Start

Select	Pick a Goldilocks word. A word that is really useful and will be encountered again.
Teach	Teach the word quickly using the STAR Topic Word Wizard. Once confident, aim for this process to take five minutes. 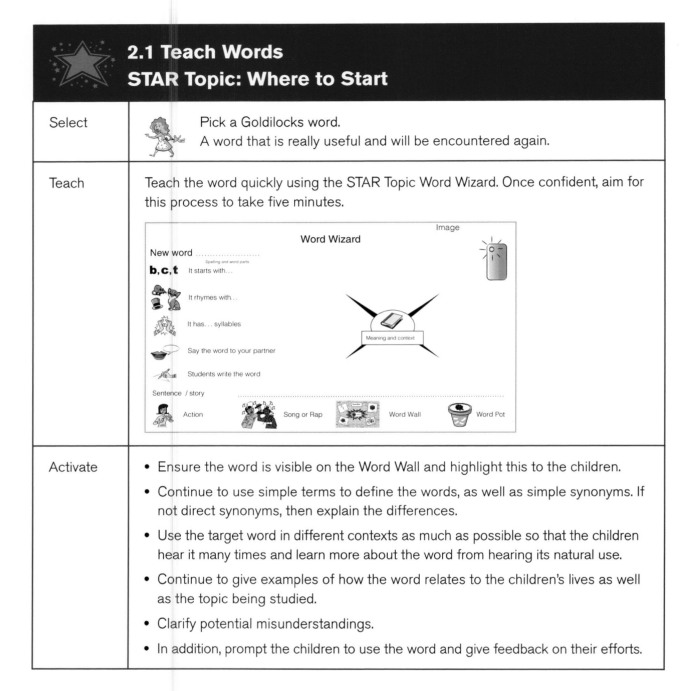
Activate	• Ensure the word is visible on the Word Wall and highlight this to the children. • Continue to use simple terms to define the words, as well as simple synonyms. If not direct synonyms, then explain the differences. • Use the target word in different contexts as much as possible so that the children hear it many times and learn more about the word from hearing its natural use. • Continue to give examples of how the word relates to the children's lives as well as the topic being studied. • Clarify potential misunderstandings. • In addition, prompt the children to use the word and give feedback on their efforts.

Review	• Review the word at the end of the lesson.
	• Play Word Wall clue games once a week, e.g. Fly swat game (see page 183)
	• Take ten words out of the Word Pot each week and talk about them (see page 191). This could be two words every day or five words twice per week.
	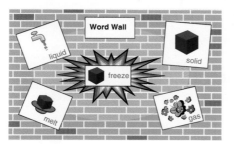 

When **starting** to use *Word Aware* begin with teaching **two words a week**. These could be either STAR Topic words or STAR Literacy or one of each. Once confident with the process then build up to teaching a word a day (**five words a week**).

References

Beck, I., McKeown, M. & Kucan, L. (2002). *Bringing Words to Life*: *Robust Vocabulary Instruction*. New York: Guilford Press.

Blachowicz, C. & Fisher, P. (2015). *Teaching Vocabulary in All Classrooms*, 5th edition. New York: Pearson.

Chiat, S. (2000). *Understanding Children with Language Problems*. Cambridge: Cambridge University Press.

Collins COBUILD Primary Learner's Dictionary (2018). Glasgow: HarperCollins.

Graves, M. (2009). *Essential Readings on Vocabulary Instruction*. Newark, DE: International Reading Association.

St. John, P. & Vance, M. (2014). Evaluation of a principled approach to vocabulary learning in mainstream classes. *Child Language Teaching and Therapy*, 30:3, 255–271.

Stahl, S. & Nagy, W. (2005). *Teaching Word Meanings*. Mahwah, NJ: Lawrence Erlbaum Associates.

Games

Pictionary (1985). Angel Games Inc.

Taboo (1989). Parker Brothers.

2.2: Teach Words: STAR Literacy

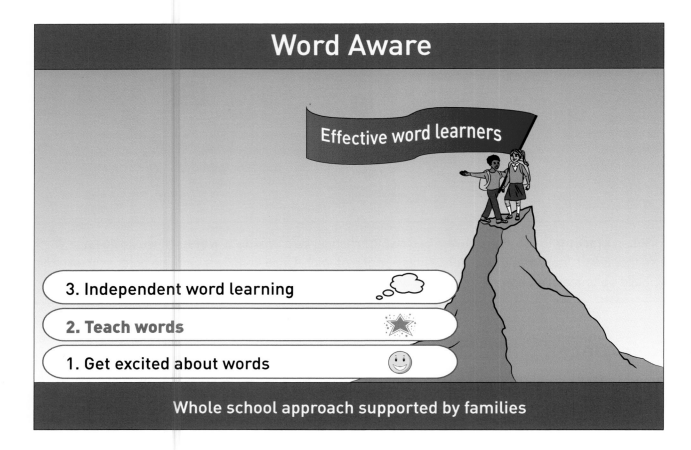

Much of the richness of both our written and spoken vocabularies is sourced from books. The more varied vocabulary used in children's literature presents a great opportunity, but it can also be a barrier, as from their oral experiences many children will not have been exposed to these more challenging words. To bridge this gap, useful words from shared books can be selected and specifically taught, thus providing children with opportunities to expand their vocabularies.

Many teachers' main motivation for vocabulary instruction is because their aim is to enrich children's writing. However, vocabulary cannot be easily compartmentalised in one subject or one domain, as words which are learnt in science will impact on writing, as will words which are learnt orally. It is therefore important to take a holistic approach to vocabulary teaching, of which direct teaching of words from shared books is one component. STAR Topic (see page 148) words are related in themes and give children access to the curriculum whereas words selected from shared books (STAR Literacy words) are more likely to be verbs or adjectives which add power and nuance to spoken and written language. The two complement each other as part of the holistic programme.

STAR Literacy can be delivered as part of an English/Literacy/Language Arts lesson and requires little equipment. If you are familiar with STAR Topic (see page 148), then STAR Literacy shares many of its features. The main difference is that the source of words is no longer prescribed by the curriculum, but instead is encountered in shared books.

The steps are as follows:

- **S**elect your shared text, ensuring it contains useful words. Then select one word at the right level to teach.
- **T**each the selected word.
- **A**ctivate the word's meaning, by guiding children to link it to their existing knowledge.
- **R**eview the taught word to ensure it is retained.

The STAR process is based on the work of Blachowicz & Fisher, 2015.

Select

Select the shared book for the whole class lesson. In our experience fiction generally offers better word choices, but non-fiction books can be used as well. Pay particular attention to the vocabulary. Is the book likely to yield words that are important for the children to know? It is worth having a look ahead as some books have surprisingly little vocabulary at the right level and others provide a rich choice.

Select: where to start

- Pick a Goldilocks word to teach. A word that is really useful and will be encountered again.

From the book select one 'Goldilocks' words, using the chart below as guidance. Of particular importance are the criteria:

- Really useful words.
- Likely to be encountered again in reading or oral language.
- Age 7+: Desirable for children to use in their writing.

Typically, when reading a whole class text, practitioners identify words because they present barriers to children accessing the text. This is necessary, but it should be noted that many of the words highlighted for this purpose are likely to be 'step on' words, and unknown to the children because they are very specific to a particular context or are rare words. *Beetle Boy* (Leonard, 2016), could be read to 8 or 9 year olds, and it contains words like 'geneticist', 'mandibles' or 'elytra' which might need to be explained but would not be the focus for in-depth teaching.

The purpose of the STAR Literacy select process is to use the whole class book as a source of vocabulary. The selected words will not be rare, and they might not even be 'wow' words. Instead we are looking for 'Goldilocks' words that once embedded can be used meaningfully in lots of different contexts. Do not spend too long deciding if a word fits the criteria, instead read on until you find one that definitely is. In most instances you do not need to read on for long until you have that 'aha' moment and find a really good 'Goldilocks' word.

With familiarity, the selection from shared books can be done during the lesson without the need for preparation. Experienced practitioners can get to the stage where they just think 'that's a good

Goldilocks word. I'll teach that in a moment.' However, it takes some time and practice to develop that skill, so in the initial stages a little advanced scanning of the next section of the shared book is advised.

Year group:	Subject:	Topic:
Anchor words	**Goldilocks words** Not too easy and not too hard, but just right	**Step on words**
Children have a thorough understanding of these words. Everyday spoken and written language for a child of this age. Used at home and in daily interactions. Children may have become familiar with this vocabulary through prior teaching.	**Really useful words** Likely to be encountered again in reading or oral language. Average adult has a **good** level of knowledge of the word. (Words that are very topic-specifc but are core to the topic.)* Age 7+: Desirable for children to use in their writing.	Less likely to be encountered again in reading or oral language. Average adult does **not have much** knowledge of the word. (Words that are particularly topic-specific and are not core to the topic.)* Age 7+: Not a word that children usually need to use in their own writing.
If a child needs to work on 'anchor' words then provide small group teaching or differentiated activities.	'Goldilocks' words will be the words that are taught to the whole class. Select one per lesson.	'Step on' words that are needed for comprehension can be briefly explained but are not the focus for in-depth teaching.

*In STAR Literacy the issue of topic words is less relevant than in STAR Topic.
(Adapted from Stahl & Nagy, 2005 and Beck et al., 2002)

Teach

After selecting the vocabulary to be taught, the next part of the STAR sequence is 'teach'.

Words which are sourced from topics will be planned and so there will be opportunity for preparation such as gathering a symbol and thinking about a child-friendly definition. The selection of words from shared texts can be done much more spontaneously, but the saved time comes at the expense of reduced preparation time.

In one lesson it is advised to teach one new 'Goldilocks' word to the whole class. This enables the word to be taught to a depth, but the teach sequence is only the beginning of the process that is then built upon

Select: example

Identifying Goldilocks words

Imagine you are the teacher of a class of 8–9 year olds and are reading *Charlotte's Web* (White, 2003) and you want to select one word to teach. There is no national or international standard for what children should know, and so this will vary according to children's experiences and abilities.

On one page (p96) there are plenty of 'anchor' words, such as 'battle', 'shining' or 'slipping' that a class of 8 or 9 year olds are likely to use as part of their everyday spoken or written language. There is also 'aeronaut' which is a 'step on' word. 'Aeronaut' might need a brief explanation but would not be a focus for teaching. There are a number of suitable candidates for 'Goldilocks' words including, **thrashing, sagging, dodging, mercilessly, lashed, swayed** and **budge**. They are all interesting and useful words that are likely to be encountered again. Class teachers would be very pleased also if these words found their way into their students' written work. Although some have more application then others **thrashing** and **lashed** are less useful than the other words. **Sagging, dodging, mercilessly, budge** and **swayed** are all potential Goldilocks words. Rather than gloss over a number of words it is recommended that one really useful word is selected for teaching, so that it can be taught to depth. **Mercilessly** (or **merciless**) is a particularly interesting and useful word to teach as it could be encountered again, but it will also add power to students' writing, and so stands out as a Goldilocks word but any of the words highlighted above may also be chosen.

Is it the best book for choosing vocabulary from?

It is important to look ahead at texts to see how many Goldilocks words they contain, as there is huge variation. For instance, *Holes* (Sachar, 2000) is a book that is widely read to 11 to 12 year olds and has many benefits for young people, however it contains very few Goldilocks words. The emphasis is often on plot and whilst students need to understand the narrative and use inference, the vocabulary is generally very simple. For instance, on one page (p6) the most demanding vocabulary was 'facing', 'contained', 'stifling', 'obstacle' and 'ratio'. Compare this selection of words to *Charlotte's Web*, which is aimed at a far younger audience. *Holes* is a great book for many reasons, but not as a source of vocabulary.

during the 'activate' and 'review' phases. By the end of the 'teach' process children do not need a complete understanding of the word's meaning, but instead a solid foundation for ongoing learning.

The teach sequence has been developed in response to what is known about how children learn words, and to be accessible for a wide range of students. It has been used in many schools internationally and proven to be easy to implement, engaging and effective.

The STAR Literacy teaching process shares many similarities with its counterpart, STAR Topic. It comes from the same principles, but these are applied in a slightly different manner. In general, the new words will be synonyms for words that the children are already familiar with as opposed to new concepts. There is a greater emphasis on understanding nuance, and discussion about when to use the new word as opposed to its synonyms. The teaching sequence can be presented and adapted according to the words being taught and the context, but the key components should remain the same.

Full details of the STAR Literacy Teach process are provided below.

Teach: where to start

Teach the word via either the Word Wizard (if you wish to write the information down, page 207) or the 'A new word in nine steps' sheet (if you would prefer to do it verbally, page 222). Both outline the same steps. Once confident, aim for either of these processes to take five minutes.

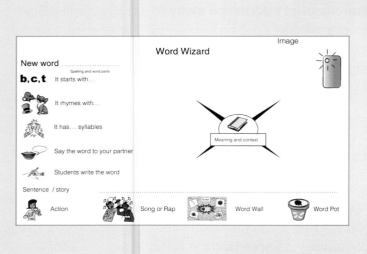

Summary of STAR Literacy teaching sequence

Full details on page 218

New word: _____ Discuss and mark spelling patterns and prefix/suffix	**The word** • Adults write the word on the Word Wizard by 'New word' or write it on the board • Underline any spelling patterns • Draw a line through the word to indicate prefix, base and suffix if applicable e.g.: New word: *trans|for|mation*
	Image Use a photograph, symbol or drawing that represents the word accompanied by the written word. Hand drawings can work well.
b, c, t	**Say and write** • clap syllables of the word as you all say it • rhyme • initial sound • say to a partner • students write the word.
	Semantics (meaning) Provide child-friendly definition, context and model how to use the word.
I like the hot and humid **climate** in India.	**Sentence and story** Look at the context from the story. Use the word in a new sentence. Tell a story where you experienced the word.
	Action Act it out where possible.

	Song Sing a song or say a rap.
	Word Wall The word and picture go on the Word Wall.
	Word Pot The word goes into the Word Pot for reviewing in the future.

To make sure you include all the key information use either the 'Word Wizard' or 'A new word in nine steps'. Completed copies of the Word Wizard can be saved for future reference. They are also available to download from the companion website.

Further detail of STAR Topic teaching sequence
The word

The target word is written on the Word Wizard or board. Discuss and underline any familiar or unfamiliar spelling patterns as the students will need to be able to use the word in their writing. It is also a time to highlight any prefixes and/or suffixes if applicable or useful. Once the prefix and suffix are highlighted, the base word will then become more obvious. Recognising words within a word is a key word learning skill. This is simply done by drawing a forward slash between different morphemes (sections of the word). It can be helpful to discuss how words can change e.g.: curious/ curiously, merciful/merciless/mercy.

motion/less	run/down
curious/ly	flour*ish*
scrump*tious*	dread/ful

Suggested markers: underline spelling patterns and indicate breaks between morphemes with a forward slash.

218

Image

If you have time, also draw a simple image. If inadequate time, then this may be added later.

Say and write

- Clap syllables: instruct the class to clap out the syllables of the word as they say the word.
- Rhyme: how many rhyming words can the class think of? These can be real or nonsense words. The purpose is that they highlight the rhyme of the target word.
- Initial sound: what speech sound does the word start with?
- Say the word to a partner: instruct the children to say the word to another child.
- Students write the word: if practical, instruct the children to write the word quickly. It can be on a whiteboard or notebook, but it may be more practical for children to write the new word at another point.

Semantics (meaning)

Define it: come up with a simple definition that uses only anchor words. Even for simple words it can be hard to generate a simple, precise definition, so model using the dictionary. The Collins COBUILD (2018) series provides straightforward definitions and a free version is available online at wwww.collinsdictionary. com. The first tab in the on-line version gives the simplest definition. Because these are simplified definitions, they do not always capture the whole meaning required, and so you may need to adapt what is in the dictionary. Be careful to keep your definition simple and include only 'Goldilocks' words.

For instance, the word **cautious** is defined under the first tab at wwww.collinsdictionary.com as:

'Someone who is **cautious** acts very carefully in order to avoid possible danger.'

The 'English' and 'American' tabs provide more complete but complex definitions, for instance for **cautious**:

'showing or having **caution**; wary; prudent'.

Even though the first definition is simpler, it is still necessary to check that both the vocabulary and grammar are accessible to the children. The word being taught is a 'Goldilocks' word and so it needs to

be defined in 'Anchor' words that the children understand. Definitions should only contain words that are easily accessible to the whole class. Sentences should be as simple and short as possible.

Synonyms come in here as well, so compare the new word to any simpler synonyms if possible. Discuss their similarities and differences, and when it is OK to use one word and not the other. Very few words are direct synonyms.

Sentence and story

- Context from the story: look back at the text you have read and discuss how the word is used in the story. Discuss why the author chose this particular word rather than a synonym. What does it add?

- Together make a new sentence using the word.

- Make up a story: some teachers are natural storytellers, but for many of us it takes practice to develop this skill. This step really helps children to remember the word, but also how and when it is appropriate to use the word. Try and make the story as engaging as possible. Make sure you use the new word and its defining synonyms, so you are explaining the definition within the story. e.g. 'I felt very **cautious** going on the high ropes. I went very carefully. I really didn't want to fall. I was going so **cautiously** my son was getting cross with me.'

Action

Act out the word where possible. Be creative. Actions may involve one child, a group or the whole class. They do not need to be formal sign language, such as Makaton. This is appropriate for both younger and older children and as well as being beneficial, it engages a wider group of word learners.

Song or rap

Sing a song or do a rap. There are songs and a rap on pages 166–168, and they are also available on You-Tube if you search 'Word Aware songs'. The lyrics can be photocopied or printed and used as prompts. The repetition of the target word within these songs helps the children to strengthen their understanding of

the word's speech sounds and hence aids memory. Children of all ages respond well to both the songs and the rap. Choose whichever ones you prefer.

Word Wall

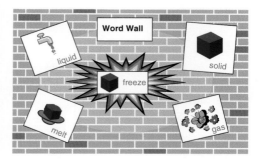

Adding the word to the Word Wall starts the 'review' segment of the STAR process. Their main purpose is to remind adults and children of the words they are learning, so they are not forgotten. Word Walls can be organised in a way that works for you in your classroom. It is a _working_ Word Wall and so the words go up as they are taught. It should be interactive, so that words that are displayed are all discussed and referred to. Placing the Word Wall at child height will facilitate them removing the words to assist with independent writing. Further guidance on creating and interacting with the Word Wall is on page 182.

Word Pot

Another key component of the 'review' part of STAR is the Word Pot. This can be any tub or box where words are easily stored and accessible. A copy of the word and image (or just the written word) on a small card is placed in the Word Pot. From time to time random words are selected from the pot and discussed briefly.

The pot can be enhanced by attaching written questions to the outside which the adult can use as prompts when reviewing words. See page 191 for further details of how to make a Word Pot and games to play to review words. Stickers with the prompt questions may also be purchased from Language for Learning:

https://www.languageforlearning.co.uk/shop/Foundation-Stage-and-Key-Stages-1-and-2/Vocabulary

In STAR Literacy the teach process can be facilitated by using the Word Wizard (see above) or you can use the 'A new word in nine steps' sheet as a prompt and do the task verbally.

A new word in nine steps

The word

New word.............

Adult writes the word.
Underline spelling patterns.
Mark prefixes/suffixes.

Image

Find an image or draw
something if you can.

Say and write

b,c,t

Clap syllables, identify
rhyme, say initial sound, and say
the word to a partner.
Students write the word.

Semantics (meaning)

Define using simple words.
Discuss synonyms.

Sentence and story

He walked **cautiously**,
trying not to fall

Look at the context in the
book. Why that word?
Make a new sentence.
Tell a story using the word.

Action

Song or rap

Word Pot

Word Wall

LEARNING WORDS

Teach example

This is an example of the STAR Literacy teaching sequence for the word **groggy**, taken from *Danny the Champion of the World* by Roald Dahl (2010, p. 150), a book suitable for 8-year olds.

The word

Spelling: Spell out the word highlighting any relevant points. 'g-r-o-g-g-y.' It has a short vowel, so there is a double 'gg'.

Morphology: 'This is funny. You can shorten the word to "grog" which is an old word for alcoholic drinks, like beer or vodka.'

Image

Write the word 'groggy' on a card together with an image. This will be added to the Word Wall later.

groggy

Say and write

Say the word 'groggy'.

Say it again and clap out and identify the number of syllables. 'Two syllables.'

Identify the first phoneme (speech sound), which is a hard 'g'.

Generate rhyming words such as 'foggy', 'doggy', 'boggy'.

If possible, children write the word on small whiteboards or in notebooks.

Semantics (meaning)

'**Groggy** means you feel a bit sleepy and confused. It can be because you have taken some medication, or you haven't had enough sleep. If you are **groggy** you might feel shaky or dizzy and you may be a bit slow to think and to move. I expect it might also be if someone has had too much to drink. They feel groggy too.'

Sentence and story

Context: In *Danny the Champion of the World* the part of the story with **groggy** in it is: '. . . there's about two hundred pheasants at this very moment roosting up in those trees and already

they're beginning to feel **groggy**. Soon they'll be falling out of the branches like raindrops!' The sleeping pills are starting to work on the pheasants and the birds are starting to feel wobbly and not steady on the branches. They are **groggy.**

Sentence: 'I hate feeling **groggy** because it means I can't think straight.'

Make up a story: 'My parents live in Australia and sometimes they get the time differences wrong. They ring me and it is very early in the morning in the UK. When I answer the phone, they say "you sound a bit **groggy**" and I say "it's because it's so early in the morning on the weekend and I haven't woken up properly!" It's hard to have a conversation when you are feeling so confused and sleepy, and rather **groggy**.'

Action

Do the following action as you say the word **groggy**. Ask the class to copy you once or twice, saying the word each time. Action: looking sleepy, confused and unsteady on your feet.

Song or rap

Sing the spell it out song all together:

Give me a **g**

Give me a **r**

Give me a **o**

Give me a **g**

Give me a **g**

Give me a **y**

Give me a/an …,
Give me a/an …,
Give me a/an …,
What does it spell?

What did it spell? **Groggy!**

Say it again? **Groggy!**

Now clap it out. **Grogg- y** (two claps)

And act it out: (Stumble about, looking dazed) **Groggy!**

And say it one more time. **Groggy!**

Word Wall

Ask a child to place the card with **groggy** on it in the starburst on the Word Wall.

Word Pot

Ask a child to write **groggy** on a small card and place it in the Word Pot.

The timing of the 'teach' sequence will vary according to practitioner preference. It is, however, perhaps most useful once the shared text has been read. This maintains the flow of the lesson and allows children to have a greater understanding of the whole text. If words are needed for comprehension they will need to be explained briefly as you go along, but the in-depth teaching may be kept to the end.

Activate

The third step in the STAR sequence is 'activate'. Activate activities will enable the child to connect the new word to his own understanding of the world. For words that have been selected from a class book there will not be the same opportunities for in-depth whole class teaching as there are for STAR Topic words, as the literacy lesson has a far broader focus than individual words. Words still need to be activated, and the key is often learning how the new word is differentiated from simpler synonyms. The aim is to facilitate children's thinking about the word and so they make the links between their own understanding of the world and the new word. For younger children (or those with limited language) this is done via activities, but for older children (and those with more language) then these links can be facilitated via questioning.

Below are a list of suggested general activities and questions, and, whilst these will support practice, the best activate questions are specific to the word. 'What does XX mean?' should be avoided, as this only requires a direct repetition of what they have just learnt. The prompt questions and activities below will be helpful as a start and will give children the opportunity to relate the new word to their existing knowledge. Some of the questions are relevant to specific parts of speech while others can be used more generally. Choose a few relevant questions for each new word. Particularly powerful is discussing how the word is similar to and different from its synonyms, as this helps children develop a greater understanding of the connections between words. Comparing word meanings requires advanced language skills and so it is not suitable for young learners or those with more limited language.

Asking for a number of answers to each question and then comparing responses will further help class members to refine their knowledge of the target words. For example, when asked 'When might someone **patrol**?' you may get one response about the police in a patrol car, another about lifeguards on a beach and a third about the neighbours' cat at night. These responses together provide richer information than each one does on its own.

Activate: where to start

Choose a few relevant questions to activate the students' understanding of the word. These questions work for any part of speech.

General	Which one of these is right? e.g.: Who would **waddle** a duck or a lion?
	Describe the word to a friend
Reflection	I like/don't like this word because . . .
	What do you learn by knowing this word?
	How does the word make you feel?

Contexts	In what kind of book or film would you see or hear this word?	
	Think of a time when you could use this word.	
	Given a context and the word, what would else would you observe? e.g.: If the house was **dilapidated**, what would you see?	
	Together, let's make two sentences which show different ways the word can be used.	
	Act out a situation which shows the meaning of the word.	
Synonyms	Think of another word that might mean something similar to this word.	
	This word is a bit like . . . How is it different from that word?	
	What's the first word that jumps into your head when you hear the new word?	
	The author chose this word . . . What other word could they have used?	
Linking	Think of three words linked to the new word.	
	If this word was a (car/animal/food) what would it be? Why?	
	By discussing children's reasons for their choices, understanding can be deepened further.	

Activate questions: more options linked to part of speech

Concrete Noun (things you can touch or see)	What can it do?
	What does it look like?
	Where might you find it?
	List three actions the object can do. Then make a phrase containing the noun and a verb.
Verb	Show me how you would do this action.
	When might someone do this? When might you do this?
	What objects might be needed to do this action?

	What animal, profession or character might do this action?
	Think of something that does that action (or is done to it) and then explain why, using 'because', 'so', 'to' or 'as', e.g. 'The train **departed** at precisely 11.14 so it would reach its destination on time.
	Think of three objects that go with this action.
Adjective	Think of something that can be described as (target word).
	What would a (insert noun) be like if it is described as (target word)?
	Think of three things that can be described as this word.
	If a person or object is described as this word, what else could you say about that person or thing?
	Adjectives often conjure up very specific atmospheres. What do you think of when you hear this word?
	Link the adjective to three nouns and then make a phrase containing the adjective and each noun, e.g.: The opulent ballroom. An opulent chandelier. The opulent decorations.
Adverb	What verb does it describe or go with? How does it change that verb?
	Act out a verb in the way the adverb tells you.
	What does this word add to the verb? How does it change it?

For examples of all these questions please see pages 236–239.

Inspired by Beck et al., 2002

Quick write

A primary aim for STAR Literacy is to enrich children's spoken and written language, so as well as talking about the words a quick written activity is beneficial. When exactly to fit writing into the flow of the lesson is an individual decision, but giving children the chance to write it once, increases the likelihood they will use it again. Here are some ideas.

Convert any of the activate questions listed above into a written task

For example: write the word **dilapidated** and then write something that could be described as **dilapidated**.

Write the new word, **hazard**, and three words which go with it.

Write the new word in three different phrases, e.g.: a shrewd decision, a shrewd manager, a shrewd look.

Or try one of these activities
Sentence completion

For this task: children copy the whole sentence (containing the word), but then add their own thoughts. e.g.:

I was woken last night by a great **howling** sound, so I went downstairs and saw . . .

Tentacles look like legs, but . . .

I expected that the journey would be **tortuous** because . . .

Rufus gave a **menacing** growl, so I went to investigate . . .

I finally asked Grandad why he looked so **mournful**, and he replied . . .

Killer sentences

Write a range of sentences containing more boring synonyms for words from the Word Wall. The task is for children to improve the sentences using the words from the Word Wall. The sentences need to be grammatically correct for both words. For example:

Word Wall words: **inconsolable**, **pondering**, **listless**, **torment**.

Sentences:

Today's day at school left me <u>thinking</u> just how many days were left until the summer holidays.

It had rained the entire week, and so I got up feeling <u>bored</u>.

The whole group looked on worried, unsure what could have made Suzie <u>sad</u>.

Each morning Zane, the school bully, would choose a child to <u>pick on.</u>

Mind map

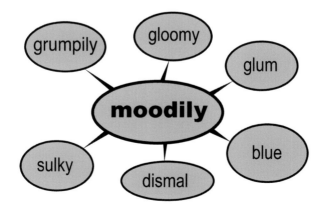

Write the word in the middle of the page and then write related words or phrases around it.

What's missing?

Each child selects a word from the Word Wall and writes a sentence but omits the target word. Others guess which word from the Word Wall fits in the missing space.

More in-depth activities to activate the word

Compare and collate

- Use the activate questions to gather a variety of answers. These can be the basis for discussion and/or displays.

- Groups generate sentences containing the target word. The group can then choose which sentence is the most interesting. Collate the chosen sentences as a class.

- For adjectives: think of objects, animals, characters or people that could be described by the target word. Draw the items and arrange on a mind map style display.

- Write the word and then draw a picture which conveys its meaning.

Make a video

Make a short video about the word. This is straightforward for verbs but can be engaging for a range of words.

Synonym Venn diagrams

Draw two interconnecting circles. Write the word and a simple synonym in each of the circles. In the centre describe the similarities. In the other part of the circle write about the differences. You can also add another circle for a third word.

Example

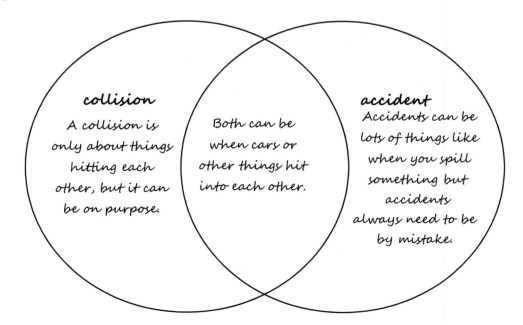

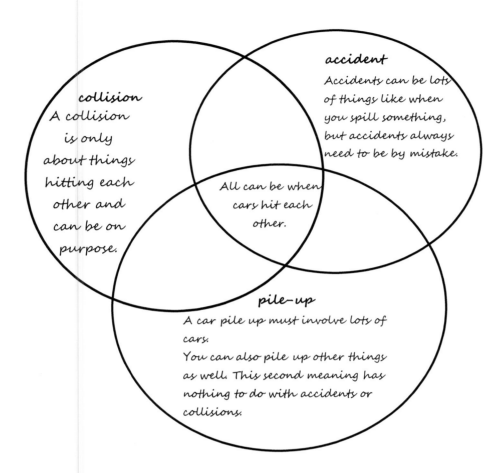

collision
A collision is only about things hitting each other and can be on purpose.

accident
Accidents can be lots of things like when you spill something, but accidents always need to be by mistake.

All can be when cars hit each other.

pile-up
A car pile up must involve lots of cars.
You can also pile up other things as well. This second meaning has nothing to do with accidents or collisions.

If a number of small groups have been set different tasks, then they can be asked to feed back to the whole class. Whichever method you choose, make sure that the children have the opportunity to talk through their thinking, link it back to their own experiences and understanding by again using the 'activate' questions above.

Activate example

Munch is a 'Goldilocks' word used in *Rumble in the Jungle* (Andreae & Wojtowycz, 2000), a book that is suitable for 6-year-olds. This word could be 'activated' using the following prompts:

- Pretend to **munch** an apple.
- Would you **munch** a sandwich or **munch** a shoe?
- When might you **munch**?

Further examples are given on pages 236–239.

Review

The final part of the STAR Literacy process is 'review'. Reviewing new words is important as it exposes children to the words again, thus giving them further opportunities to develop an understanding of the word and assimilate it into their vocabularies, as well as ensuring that the word is not forgotten. It is quick and easy to do.

Review the word at the end of the lesson

Talk about the word again and review what has been learnt by asking a few questions along the lines of: 'What was the word again?', 'During the lesson, what did you learn about the word?', 'Let's all clap the word together' and 'Let's act the word together'. Encourage students to take responsibility for their word learning by asking them, 'When do you think you might use this word again?' and 'Tell the person next to you how you will remember the word.'

> What was that word again?

Notice and use the word at other times

Children develop understanding of words over time, so teaching staff should endeavour to use the target words in different contexts. Does it all get a bit **frantic** at some point in the day and could any student's behaviour be described as **listless**? Use the Word Wall as a prompt to remind teaching staff to use the words in context as the opportunities arise. Also encourage classroom visitors, including headteachers/principals to use the target words.

> Oh, you are **frantic**. You look in a rush to finish.

Use words in independent writing

Encourage children to use the words in their writing. Prompt them to take the word off the Word Wall and place it on their desks in order to assist with spelling. Notice and praise when children use the target words in their writing.

Transparent

Listen out for the word tally

One successful strategy is a class tally chart to record when children identify words that they have heard (Beck et al., 2002). To be credited with a point a child needs to be able to describe the sentence and the context in which they encountered the word. It does not matter if they make it up because the formulation of any response requires active processing. Record on the 'Listen out for the word tally' sheet. See below. A printable version is available on the companion website.

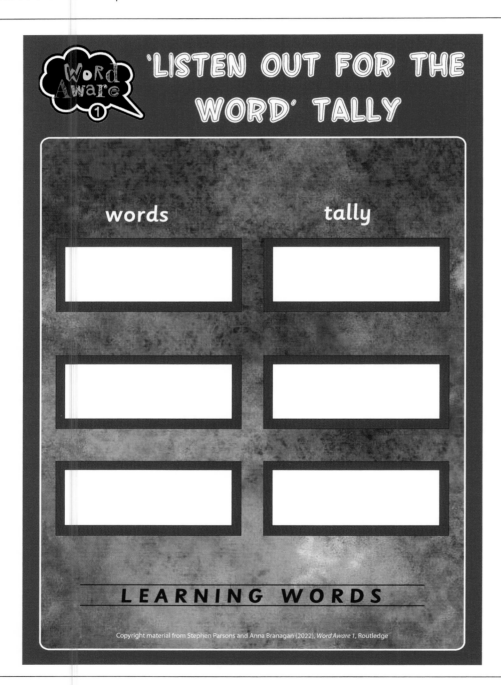

Word Aware 1

'LISTEN OUT FOR THE WORD' TALLY

words	tally

LEARNING WORDS

Add the writing to a new word book

Establish a new word book for each child to record the words they have learnt. The 'Word summary' (page 196) or 'Reflections on word learning' (page 197) may be used, or a blank page in an exercise book with children encouraged to record their understanding by writing or drawing.

Synonym match

Select a range of words from the Word Pot or Word Wall and display them at the front of the class. The children then select one of these words and writes this on a card. On a separate card each child writes a synonym for their chosen word. Once you have a set, mix them up and scatter them on the table. Children take turns to match each word to its synonym.

Use any of the review games described in STAR topic review games

(pages 182–204)

Word Wall games	Word Pot games	Creative review games	Homework
Word Wall clue games (including 'fly swat' and 'it's behind you') Say it in a sentence Collecting class knowledge Connections Word Wall review cards Reverse review cards Word spinner Reflections on word learning	Connect 2 As quick as you can Against the clock Mini bingo Shaboo Quick quiz	One-word book Word summary Word mind map True or False folding books Vocabulator Fortune teller Magic book	Fridge Words Stickers Context challenge Word expert

Review

The word **munch** is reviewed at the end of the session. Everyone pretends to munch their favourite food. The class is given stickers with a picture of someone eating and the words 'Talk to me about the word **munch**'. The lunchtime supervisors see the word **munch** and comment that the children are really **munching** their food today. They have conversations with family members about the word **munch** that evening. The class has a temporary teacher in the next day who sees the word **munch** on the Word Wall. She wonders aloud what the word means. One of the children explains what it means. The whole class does the action that accompanies the word.

2.2 Teach Words
STAR Literacy: Where to start summary

Select

Pick a Goldilocks word.
A word that is really useful and will be encountered again.

Teach

Teach the word via either the Word Wizard (if you want to write the information down, page 172) or the 'A new word in nine steps' sheet (if you would prefer to do it verbally, page 222). Once confident, aim for either of these processes to take five minutes.

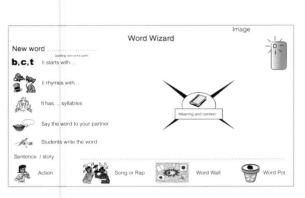

Activate

Choose a few relevant questions to activate the students' understanding of the word. These questions work for any word type.

General	Which one of these is right? e.g.: Who would **waddle**, a duck or a lion?
	Describe the word to a friend
Reflection	I like/don't like this word because . . .
	What do you learn by knowing this word?
	How does the word make you feel?

Contexts	In what kind of book or film would you see or hear this word?
	Think of a time when you could use this word.
	Given a context and the word, what would else would you observe? e.g.: If the house was **dilapidated**, what would you see?
	Together, let's make two sentences which show different ways the word can be used.
	Act out a situation which shows the meaning of the word.
Synonyms	Think of another word that might mean something similar to this word.
	This word is a bit like . . . How is it different from that word?
	What's the first word that jumps into your head when you hear the new word?
	The author chose this word . . . What other word could they have used?
Linking	Think of three words linked to the new word.
	If this word was a (car/animal/food), what would it be? Why?
	By discussing children's reasons for their choices understanding can be deepened further.

Review

- Review the word at the end of the lesson
- Play a Word Wall game at least once a week, e.g. Fly swat game (see page 183)
- Take ten words out of the Word Pot each week and talk about them (see page 192).

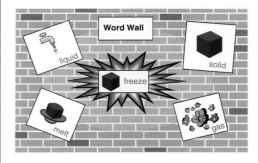

When **starting** to use *Word Aware* begin with teaching **two words a week**. These could be either STAR Topic words or STAR Literacy or one of each. Once confident with the process then build up to teaching a word a day (**five words a week**).

Activate questions with examples

All word types

	Activity	Examples
General	Which one of these is right?	'Which would you describe as **grotesque**? A ballerina or a zombie?' 'What would someone do to you if they were **malicious**? Would they deface your schoolbooks or give you a gift?'
	Describe the word to your friend.	'**Treachery** is an evil word. It is when someone has done something really bad. They hurt someone who trusted them.'
Reflection	I like/don't like this word because . . .	'I don't like the word **anxiously**, as it makes me feel bad.' 'I like the word **suspicious** because I like how the word sounds.'
	What do I learn by knowing this word?	'By knowing the word **rotund** I can talk about someone being fat, a bit more politely.'
	How does the word make you feel?	'When it is **drizzling** outside, it makes me feel depressed.' 'If someone told me I looked **elegant** I would laugh.'
Contexts	In what kind of book or film would you see or hear this word?	'I might see the word **nourishing** in a cookbook', 'I might hear **mournful** in a film about war.'
	Think of a time when you could use this word	'I would use the word **creep** when I was talking about how to surprise someone.'
	In the book it was used like this, but it can be used like this too	'In the story they talked about the campaign building **momentum**, but a ball or a rock rolling down a hill can also gain **momentum**.'
	Given a context and the word, what would else would you observe?	If the house was **dilapidated**, what would you see? If you were in a restaurant and there was a **feast**, what would you see? If children were in a class and they were **fascinated**, what would the children be doing?
	Together, let's make two sentences which show different ways the word can be used.	'I heard about the police **incident** in Worcester. There was an **incident** in the playground between two Year 5 children.'

	Act out a situation which shows the meaning of the word.	Students talk to each other in a **suspicious** manner, breaking off conversation whenever anyone else comes within earshot.
Synonyms	Think of another word that might mean something similar to this word.	'Threatening is a bit like **menacing**.'
	This word is a bit like . . . How is it different from that word?	'**Fascinated** is a bit like interested, but I think **fascinated** is when you are really interested and trying to work something out.'
	What's the first word that jumps into your head when you hear the word?	'What's the first word that jumps into your head when you hear **opportunity**? For me it is chance.'
	The author chose this word. What other word could they have used?	The author used the word **clambering.** What other word could they have used?
Linking	Three words linked to the new word.	**Hazard**: danger, warning, ouch! **Teeming**: people, insects, rain. **Envy**: greedy, money, want.
	If this word was a (car/ animal/food), what would it be? Why?	'If **gasped** was a car it would be a Porsche, as Porsches look amazing and make you gasp.' 'If **knowledge** was an animal it would be an owl as they are very wise.' 'If **teeming** was an animal, it would be ants because there are always lots of them and they get everywhere.'

Concrete Noun (things you can touch or see)	What can it do?	'An **urchin** might be on the streets and be looking for food to eat.'
	What does it look like?	'**Tentacles** look like legs, but they are bendy.'
	Where might you find it?	'You find a **brim** on a hat.'
	List three actions the object can do or what can be done with it. Then make a phrase containing the noun and a verb.	'The **guardian** is protecting. The **guardian** is looking after the children. The **guardian** is locking the doors.'

Verb	Show me how you would do this action.	'Show me how you walk along and then **halt**.'
	When might someone do this? When might you do this?	'Someone might **howl** when they are really upset or really don't like something.' 'I might **scowl** when I really don't like something but can't say it out loud.'
	What objects might be needed to do this action?	'To **capture** an animal, you might need a net or a pen to put it in.'
	What animal or profession might do this action?	'A horse **prances**', 'A head teacher **bellows**', 'A chick **emerges**', 'An explorer **discovers**.'
	Think of something that does that action (or is done to it) and then explain why, using 'because', 'so', 'to' or 'as'.	'The train **departed** so it would be on time', 'The motorcyclist **winced** as the glass was removed from his arm', 'I was **guzzling** my food because I was hungry'.
	Think of three things that go with this action.	'**Beckon** makes me think of a teacher, a curled finger and a witch.' '**Quivering** makes me think of fear, cold and feeling small.'
Adjective	Can you think of something that can be described as (target word)?	'Old rooms can sometimes be **dingy** if they haven't been looked after and kept clean'
	What would a (insert noun) be like if it is described as (target word)?	'What would popcorn be like if it was **irre-sistible**? It would smell buttery and be glistening under the lights and would be very fresh. **Irresistible!**'
	Think of three things that can be described as this word.	'**Defective.** 'The old computer, the light and the projector are all **defective**. None of them work.' '**Gloomy**. A dark room, a cave, an old church.'
	If an object or person is described as this word, what else could you say about that person or thing?	'If you describe someone as **mysterious**, what else could you say about them? A **mysterious** person might be acting in an unusual way or might even not be seen much at all but doing things that interest other people.'

	Adjectives often conjure up very specific atmospheres. What do you think of when you hear this word?	'When I hear the word **solitary,** I think of someone who is all alone. They are lonely and sad.'
	Link the adjective to three objects and then make phrases containing each adjective.	'The **encouraging** words, the **encouraging** noises and the **encouraging** smile.'
Adverb	What verb does it describe or go with? How does it change that verb?	**'Suspiciously** might go with "look". It means that you look in a way that shows that you don't trust what you see.'
	Act out a verb in the way the adverb tells you.	'Pick up this pen **reluctantly**.'
	What does this word add to the verb? How does it change it?	'Receiving the gift **appreciatively** is different to just receiving the gift. Tell me how.'

Inspired by Beck et al., 2002

Activate examples related to specific books and related words, targeted at different age groups

Words from *Rumble in the Jungle* (Andreae & Wojtowycz, 2000) suitable for 6-year-olds.

Wander	• When might you **wander**? • Would you **wander** when you are late or when you have lots of time? • **Wander** is a bit like 'walk'. How is it different from 'walk'?
Ferocious	• What animal might be **ferocious**? • Would you like to meet a **ferocious** animal? Why? Why not? • Do you like the word **ferocious**? Why? Why not?
Tremble	• Can you think of a time when you might **tremble**? • Finish this: 'I walked into the house and **trembled** because . . .' • What story or TV programme makes you **tremble**?
Prowling	• What animal might **prowl**? • Let's all **prowl** like a tiger. • What is the tiger looking for when it is **prowling**?

Words taken from *Danny the Champion of the World* (Dahl, 2010), suitable for 8-year-olds.

Snuffle	• What animal might **snuffle**? • Describe **snuffle** to your friend. • Think of a time when you could use the word **snuffle**.
Gaze	• When might someone **gaze**? • The author chose the word **gaze**. What other word could he have used? Which one is better? • How is **gaze** different from **look**?
Permitted	• I am going to select two children to act out a short play. One is going to be a parking inspector and one is going to be a driver who has parked in the wrong place. Let's all think how the parking inspector can use the word **permitted**. • What things are **permitted** in school? What things are not **permitted**? • Think of a time you might use the word **permitted**.
Repulsive	• Act out holding something that is **repulsive**. What is it? What does it look, smell and feel like? • What food do you think is **repulsive**? • Think of three things that can be described as **repulsive**. What attribute do they share? '**Repulsive** smell. **Repulsive** snotty tissue. **Repulsive** slimy food. They are all disgusting and make me want to be sick.'

Words selected from *Kensuke's Kingdom* (Morpurgo, 1999), suitable for 10- to 11-year-olds.

Tormentor	• If someone is a **tormentor** what might they do? • Do you know any fictional characters who are **tormentors**? • If you describe someone as a **tormentor** what else could you say about them?
Listlessly	• What verb does **listlessly** describe or go with? How does it change that verb? (e.g.: **listlessly** goes with 'walked'. It slows it down, makes it lazy.) • Pretend you are brushing your hair **listlessly**. • If you were moving **listlessly**, do you think you would like to have a rest or go for a run?

Pondering	• Can you think of a word that is a bit like **pondering**? How is this word different from **pondering**? (e.g.: it's a bit like thinking but is slower and more careful.)
	• Pretend to **ponder** about what you might like to have for dinner.
	• Can cars **ponder**? Can cats **ponder**? Can head teachers/ principals **ponder**?
Inconsolable	• What might make you be **inconsolable**?
	• If a baby is **inconsolable**, does he cry for a short time or a long time? Is the crying loud or quiet?
	• Pretend to tell your friend that your favourite game is broken. Your friend tries to mend it but you are **inconsolable**.

References

Andreae, G. & Wojtowycz, D. (2000). *Rumble in the Jungle*. London: Orchard Books.

Beck, I., McKeown, M. & Kucan, L. (2002). *Bringing Words to Life*: *Robust Vocabulary Instruction*. New York: Guilford Press.

Blachowicz, C. & Fisher, P. (2015). *Teaching Vocabulary in All Classrooms*, 5th edition. New York: Pearson.

Collins COBUILD Primary Learner's Dictionary (2018). London: HarperCollins.

Dahl, R. (2010). *Danny the Champion of the World*. London: Puffin Books.

Leonard, M. G. (2016). *Beetle Boy*. Frome, Somerset: Chicken House.

Morpurgo, M. (1990). *Kensuke's Kingdom*. London: Heinemann.

Sachar, L. (2000). *Holes*. London: Bloomsbury.

Stahl, S. & Nagy, W. (2005). *Teaching Word Meanings*. Mahwah, NJ: Lawrence Erlbaum Associates.

White, E. B. (2003). *Charlotte's Web*. London: Penguin Books.

Independent Word Learning

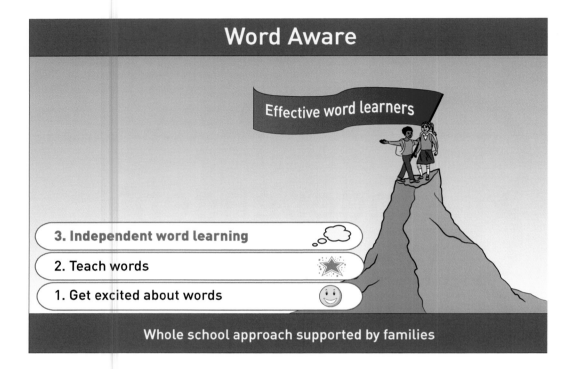

As educators, we can encourage children's interest in words and teach them specific words, but most vocabulary will be learnt independently, as they read independently and follow their own interests. And so, the third step in the *Word Aware* process is to develop independent word learning skills, so that the children we teach are enabled to learn words when they read, consume media and talk to others.

The first step ('Get Excited About Words', page 28) helped to build an enriched word-learning environment that was fun and motivating. The second step ('Teach Words', page 148) ensured that children had a strong knowledge of useful and important words. Both of these steps will have indirectly developed children's independent word learning skills, but by explicitly teaching these skills we can ensure our students have the skills they need to take them into the future.

There is evidence that teaching word learning strategies can have a positive impact on vocabulary growth (White et al., 2009; Graves, 2004). In their systematic review of the literature Ford-Connors and Paratore (2015) highlight three key independent word learning strategies which impact on word learning: context clues, morphological analysis and polysemy (multiple meaning words) awareness. For context clues the authors noted 'the more effective instruction included teaching students to examine words and sentences that precede or follow the unknown word and to seek relationships among ideas across sentences or paragraphs to infer a general idea about the new word's meaning'. (p.69). This strategy is reflected in the common classroom instruction to 'read around the word'.

Morphological analysis is noted as a key skill by a number of other researchers also. Nippold and Sun (2008) highlight that this skill becomes increasingly important from the top end of primary/elementary school onwards as words that children encounter become more morphologically complex. Sparks and Deacon (2015) found that vocabulary growth between Grades 2 and 3 was predicted by the children's skills with analysing morphology (a key word learning skill) rather than the size of their vocabulary in Grade 2. Ford-Connors and Paratore (2015) conclude that 'morphological analysis provided a valuable tool to help students with and without disabilities to unlock word meanings. . . . students improved both knowledge of words and ability to infer meanings from new words'. (p.72).

The third skill area identified by Ford-Connors and Paratore (2015) is awareness of polysemy. They identify that many others have highlighted words with multiple meanings being problematic for many learners, including those who speak English as an Additional Language (EAL)/English Language Learners (ELL). However, there are very few studies investigating the effectiveness of teaching children about polysemous words, but it is important to address as most common English words have multiple meanings.

Underpinning the Teach Words component of *Word Aware* is a systematic approach to structuring phonology, grammar and word meaning. These are foundation skills, but other crucial vocabulary skills include ability to use words in sentences, definition skills and awareness of word learning strategies. Benelli et al. (2006) highlight how children's ability to define skills enables word learning, and so these skills should also be specifically taught.

In general, independent word learning strategies become increasingly important as children encounter more words through their own reading. The children with the most developed word learning strategies will be able to understand more of what they read, build their vocabulary and reading comprehension (Levesque et al., 2019). Rastle (2019) adds that independent word learning strategies not only promote reading comprehension but also spelling. Many of the skills targeted in this section of the book will impact on literacy as well, but the primary focus is word meaning.

Do not wait until children are independent readers to teach them strategies. Lyster et al. (2016) taught pre-school children about morphological rules and found that it had an impact several years later. Most children start using word learning strategies at a relatively early age, as they will have a natural interest in words and spontaneously ask, 'What does that mean?' when they hear a novel word. However, not all strategies are applicable to young children as conscious word learning requires children to be able to reflect on their own learning. Strategies will need to be introduced when developmentally appropriate and revisited a number of times over several years before they are truly embedded.

Teaching Independent Word Learning Skills

To be a successful word learner, children need to have a range of strategies that they can apply independently to work out the meanings of words. This process needs to be introduced and added to over a period of several years as children become developmentally ready for each skill. As curriculum and vocabulary demands increase, the application needs to also become more sophisticated. Teaching word learning skills is a long-term process and taught skills may not have an immediate impact on vocabulary growth, but the expectation is that they will in the long term.

Teaching independent word learning skills sits most naturally within the literacy/language arts strand of the curriculum, but opportunities will arise in all subject areas. For instance, 82% of academic words have a Greek or Latin basis (Coxhead, 2000) and so science and mathematics will offer many opportunities. Unknown words can come from virtually any source, so it is a cross-curricular skill. Whilst much of

the research applies to reading, a focus on oral language is crucial for all learners, as throughout life we continue to learn words from what we hear.

Key Skills of Effective Word Learners

Research and best practice have been condensed into the following key skills required to become an effective word learner. 'Supporting others' word learning' has been added because the child doing the explaining is reinforcing their own skills, so is mutually beneficial, but also because this contributes to a class culture of word learning.

A. Show an interest in words

B. Identify words that are not understood

C. Word learning foundation skills

D. Work out words' meanings

E. Find out about unknown words

F. Remember and use new words

G. Support others' word learning

On the following pages are activities to promote and track the development of these skills. Some children in your class will have many of these skills in place already, but a step-by-step process will ensure that a greater percentage of the class develop these skills, but also that the children will learn how to talk explicitly about these skills and support each other.

Whole Class Approach to Developing Independent Word Learning Skills

 Independent Word Learning: Where to Start

- Make a judgement about class's word learning skills using the checklists on page 247 for children under 7 and the one on page 249 if they are over 7.
- Choose one area to focus on. Choose a strategy that you ticked 'some' children as already using.
- Teach strategies to the whole class.
- Embed strategies into day-to-day conversations.
- Move on to the next skill and repeat.

Make a judgement about class's word learning skills

Reflect upon the whole class's skills: use the rating scales below to make a judgement. If unsure of any responses, spend time sampling or observing the class or trial a whole class activity from those listed below.

Level 1: Whole Class Independent Word Learning Skills for Beginner Readers (Typically Under 7)

Class .... Date.................................

Area	Skill	Few	Some	Almost all
1. We are interested in words	Show an interest in words in spoken language and books.			
	Show pride in words that have been learnt.			
2. We think about words we don't understand	Understand that no one knows all of the words and that different people know different words.			
	If asked, they can reliably say if they know the meaning of a word or if they don't.			
3. We have lots of skills that help us with new words	When given a word, can say what the first sound is, how many syllables it has and what the word rhymes with.			
	Can look within words they hear and identify compound word components (e.g. bath/room) and common suffixes such as '-ed', '-ing', '-s'.			
	Are aware of dictionaries, thesauri, glossaries and Word Walls.			
	Understand that words have multiple meanings.			
	Can give simple definitions for common nouns.			

Area	Skill	Few	Some	Almost all
4. We know what to do to try and work out what a word means	<u>When being read to</u>, apply background, picture or text knowledge to work out a word's meaning.			
5. We find out about new words	Will ask someone if they don't know what a word means.			
6. We remember and use new words	Use words encountered in books, in spoken language.			
7. We help other people learn new words	Talk to peers about word meanings, and able to provide simple definitions.			

Level 2: Whole Class Independent Word Learning Skills for Established Readers (Typically Aged 7+)

Class .... Date...............................

Area	Skill	Few	Some	Almost all
1. We are interested in words	Show an interest in words in spoken language and books.			
	Show pride in words they have learnt independently.			
2. We think about words we don't understand	Understand that no one knows all of the words and that different people know different words.			
	Will independently identify words that they do not know the meaning of.			
	In reading, will spontaneously stop when they encounter a word they do not know.			
3. We have lots of skills that help us with new words	Able to identify nouns, verbs, adjectives and adverbs.			
	Can identify a range of prefixes, suffixes and root words, use them to build words and discuss how they change a word's meaning and use.			
	Able to use dictionaries, thesauri, glossaries and Word Walls to support word learning.			
	Understand that words have multiple meanings.			
	Able to define known words clearly.			
	Able to articulate own word learning strategies.			

Area	Skill	Few	Some	Almost all
4. We know what to do to try and work out what a word means	Spontaneously re-reads sections of text to work out a word's meaning.			
	Spontaneously able to identify part of speech (e.g. noun) and looks within words (e.g. prefixes) to work out a word's meaning.			
	Able to talk through strategies used to work out what words mean.			
5. We find out about new words	Will ask someone if they don't know what a word means.			
	Independently uses dictionaries, thesauri and glossaries to look up words (paper-form or online).			
	When words have multiple meanings, able to select the appropriate definition for a word.			
6. We remember and use new words	Has a method for recording new words they want to remember.			
	Use words that have been learnt spontaneously when writing and speaking.			
7. We help other people learn new words	For familiar words, able to define words in a way that is helpful to others.			
	Able to show others how to use word learning tools such as dictionaries.			

This rating scale does not address issues of decoding. The assumption here is that children have mastered phonics and are not guessing because they cannot decode words.

Decide a whole class target

Once you are confident with your judgement, select a word learning target for the whole class. If only 'some' or 'few' children are interested in words, then this is the place to start. Otherwise, start with a skill that 'some' children in the class have acquired. As a result of this process you may become aware of some children who need greater support for their word learning skills. Extra support may often be provided via including the activities in existing small group work, such as guided reading.

Introduce 'Word Detective' to the class

Introduce the 'Becoming a Word Detective' poster on page 252.

Introduce 'What Word Detective skills do we have?' (page 253). Put a big tick next to the skills that the class have established. Emphasise all the great skills the class has. On the sheet, circle one skill that was selected to focus on developing (from the 'some' column) and introduce this. This will be the starting point for teaching.

Teach 'Word Detective' to the class

Use the activities in this part of the book to teach the selected skill. Each activity is either a level 1 (approximately under 7 years) or a level 2 (approximately over 7 years) or is suitable for both. Pick the appropriate level for your class. These levels are made as a general guide and can be adapted as necessary.

Model how the skill is applied in everyday situations, such as whole class discussion or small group reading.

Use the summary worksheets for each skill to allow children to reflect upon their learning.

Once the skill has been learnt then this element gets a big tick on the 'What Word Detective skills do we have?' and another skill can be identified.

Suggestions for continued development are provided at the end of each section, but occasional opportunities to apply the specifically taught skills are beneficial.

Becoming a Word Detective

Detectives need tools such as magnifying glasses, notebooks and gloves in their bag. They use these to look for clues at a crime scene. Just like a crime detective, a 'word detective' goes looking for and finding out things. But the things they find out are words. There are one million words in the English language so there are always more words to find out about.

We are all going to be word detectives! But to be a brilliant word detective we need to have lots of tools in our bag. Let's have a look at what we have inside our word detective bag already.

What Word Detective Skills Do We Have?

1. We are interested in words

2. We can talk about words we don't understand

3. We have lots of skills that help us with new words (e.g. meaning, parts of words, using dictionaries)

4. We know what to do to try and work out what a word means

5. When we don't know a word, we can ask someone what it means

6. We remember and use new words

7. We help other people learn new words

1. We are Interested in Words

If 'few' or 'some' children aren't engaged, interested and excited by words it is really important to spend time going back to Step 1: Get Excited About Words (page 28) and get more of the class motivated. Spend at least six weeks on this before doing any other Word Detective strategies.

Level	Skill	Activities
1 & 2	Shows an interest in words in spoken language and books	• Read a story to the class, stop and talk about interesting words, encourage them to select words they like. • All children nominate a word they like and provide reasons. Extend with drawings and displays. • Select stories or poetry with alliteration, onomatopoeia or rhyme. Enjoy the sounds of words and encourage participation. • Use activities from 'Step 1: Get Excited About Words' e.g.: Authors' words, the Gift of Words, Draw your favourite word, Why that word?, Story connections, Important words, 'Word Collector' bookmarks, 'Finding different words' bookmarks, and My treasure chest words (pages 92–94). • Play word games (pages 123–146). • Collecting words: Give groups of children a word collection challenge. It might be specific, for example, words to describe the Arctic regions, verbs used to describe how robots move or adjectives to describe Queen Victoria. Children can brainstorm ideas, use sources such as non-fiction books, thesauri or the web. They can then refine their selection into their most powerful words, which can be further refined in whole class discussion. • Level 2: Teach etymology (the history of words). Many words have interesting and even bizarre stories behind them. Resources such as the *Oxford School Dictionary of Word Origins* (Ayto, 2009) are useful. Etymonline.com provides definitive answers, but they may be hard for children to decipher. Here are some words with interesting etymology to capture children's attention: atlas, badminton, ballet, biscuit, bonfire, bus, carnivorous, crocodile, custard, denim.

1 & 2	Shows pride in words that have been learnt I learnt a new word today	• When a child learns a new word independently reward verbally or with stickers: 'I learnt a new word today'. • Whole class learning can be reinforced with any of the review games (page 183–204). • Keep a class record when newly learnt words are used. Record on the 'Listen out for the word tally' (page 181). • Level 2: Use 'I am interested in words' on page 256.

Continue to develop these skills

- Hold whole school vocabulary events (see page 28 for inspiration).
- Select books with interesting vocabulary and appreciate and discuss authors' choices of words.
- Play word games.
- Any activity which celebrates words.

Level 2

Name .... **Date** ....

I am Interested in Words

Words I like the sound of

Words I have learnt

Words I like the meaning of

A word I would like to remember is

I can use it when

2.   We Think About Words We Don't Understand

Level	Skills	Activities
1 & 2	Understands that no one knows all of the words and that different people know different words.	• Level 1 & 2: Set it up with yourself and another familiar adult to ask each other words that one knows but the other does not, and vice versa. Emphasise the point that no one knows all of the words. Discuss a range of words that some children will know more than others. • Level 1 & 2: Children write a list of (or talk about) words associated with a special interest. Use the 'Special words I know' on page 259. Compare words known and discuss. • Level 2: Children use the 'Staff survey: What words do you know?' (page 260). Discuss differences.
1 & 2	Can identify words they don't know the meaning of and rate their knowledge. **Understanding words** Never heard of it Heard of it but not sure what it means Know what it means	• Level 1 & 2: Display the self-rating scale 'Understanding words' (page 262) and refer to it when discussing new vocabulary. • Level 1 & 2: Alternately use a thumbs up/sideways/down for children to indicate level of knowing a word. • Level 1 & 2: Read a short text to the class. Talk about how there will often be words we do not understand. Then ask children to click their fingers when there is a word they do not understand. Give praise when children identify unknown words. • Level 1 & 2: When starting a new topic, ask children to rate their own knowledge of key words. Use 'How much do I know?' (level 2) on page 264 or thumbs up/sideways/down (level 1 & 2).

		I asked about a new word	• Level 1 & 2: If you have another adult in your class, ask them to record any unknown words they hear. These could be words that they genuinely do not know or words that they think the children might not know. • Level 1 & 2: Identify a child to be the 'New word monitor'. Start with children with a broader vocabulary and then rotate the role. Their role is similar to the above, and to identify words that the class may not know. • Level 1 & 2: Use stickers 'I asked about a new word'. • Level 2: Homework task: parents read text to their children, who click their fingers when children hear a word they do not know. Parents are encouraged to support via homework task. See page 263.
1 & 2	In reading, will spontaneously stop when they encounter a word they do not know.		• Level 1 & 2: Model stopping when an unknown word is encountered. • Level 2: Copy a page of text. Instruct children to underline words they do not understand. • Level 2: Before starting any comprehension exercise, ask children to underline any words they don't understand. This can be in any subject. • Level 2: During independent reading, all students are instructed to select one word they do not know and write it on a sticky note. Display the words and discuss. • Level 2: Summarise learning with 'I look out for words' on page 265.

Continue to develop these skills

• 'Think aloud' when you encounter words you do not know and just comment 'I'm not sure I know what that word means' or similar.

• Encourage students to rate their own level of knowledge of new words.

• From time to time instruct students to go looking for words they do not know.

Level 1 & 2

Name: .... **Date:** ....

Special Words
I Know

Think about something you know a lot about. It could be sailing, games, football, ballet, programming, Judo, Marvel heroes or Harry Potter. It doesn't matter what the topic is, but you do need to know lots about it. Write five special words about that topic.

Topic: _____

Special words:

1.

2.

3.

4.

5.

259

Level 2

Name: .... **Date:** ....

Staff Survey: What Words do You Know?

Ask the teachers about how well they know each of these words. Tell them it is ok if they don't know what the words mean: we all know different words.

They know it: ✔   **They aren't sure:** ?   **They don't know it:** ✖

		Teachers' names						
Computers	vlogger							
	router							
	hyperlink							
	bytes							
Music	musical chord							
	ensemble							
	harmony							
	octave							

		Teachers' names						
Medical	thoracis							
	ocular							
	urology							
	intestine							
Politics	anarchy							
	autocracy							
	gerrymandering							
	bipartisan							

Self Rating Scale

UNDERSTANDING WORDS

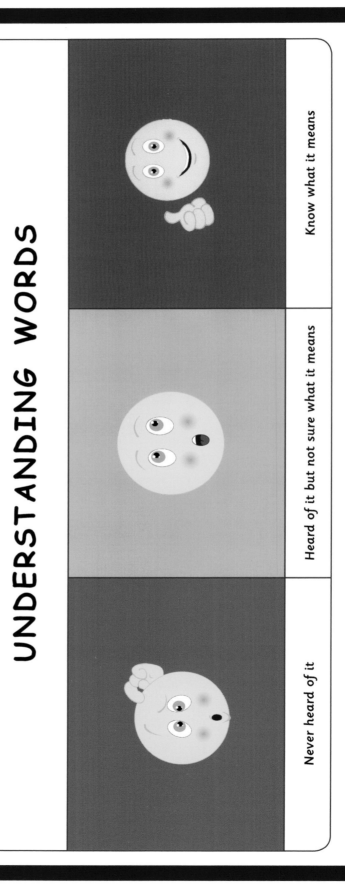

| Never heard of it | Heard of it but not sure what it means | Know what it means |

Level 2

Homework Task: Which Words Don't I Understand?

The aim is for families to identify words they do not know and talk about them.

Step 1: find a short article that will be of interest to your child, but that also contains some more challenging words. Online news websites or BBC Bitesize are a good place to start. Your child's teacher can give you some suggestions.

Step 2: explain to your child that the article might contain some hard words, and their job is to listen out for the words and click their fingers when they hear any words they are not sure they understand.

Step 3: read the article to your child. Read it slowly and stop a little longer between sentences. Prompt your child to click their fingers and join in when there are words you are not sure about. When your child clicks their fingers, stop and discuss word meanings.

If you are unsure what the word means, then look it up on your phone, as a key learning point is no one knows all of the words. Use online dictionaries such as www.collinsdictionary.com.

If your child does not identify words, then either they need more encouragement, or your article is too easy.

This task does not need to be done in English. Read an article in any language you and your child are confident in.

Level 2

How Much Do I Know?

Name: .... Date: ....

Look at the words your teacher has given you. Tick the box saying how much you know about the word. There is no right or wrong answer as we all know different words. We have given you an example.

Words	Never heard of it	Heard of it but not sure what it means	Know what it means
Example: *dilapidated*		✔	

Level 2

Name: .... Date: ....

I Look Out for Words

Give yourself a tick after you have completed each example.

☐ I know that no one knows all of the words. We know different words from each other.

☐ I knew this word......................... some of my friends/my teacher didn't know it.

☐ My friends/my teacher knew this word................................. I didn't know it.

☐ To find out more about the word I . . .

☐ When someone is talking, I listen out for words I don't know. I did this when . . .

☐ A word I learnt about when someone was talking was . . .

☐ When reading I can find words I do not know the meaning of. I did this on . . .

☐ A word I learnt about when I was reading was . . .

3. We Have Lots of Skills that Help us With New Words

Level	Skills	Activities
1	Can identify initial phoneme (speech sound), syllable and rhyme.	• Emphasise these as part of how we learn words using the 'Word Wizard' or 'A new word in nine steps'. • Develop phonological awareness skills orally such as rhyme games, identifying initial phonemes and clapping syllables. • Phonics teaching.
1	Can look within words and identify • compound word components • common suffixes such as -ed, -ing, -s	• A more in-depth description of teaching morphological awareness is available on page 269, with accompanying activities on pages 273 to 281. **Prefix** **mis**understanding **Root** mis**understand**ing **Suffix** misunderstand**ing**
2	Can identify a range of prefixes, suffixes and root words, use them to build words and discuss how they change the word's meaning and use	
2	Able to identify **nouns**, **verbs** adjectives and **adverbs** **Part of speech** **Noun** — ball **Verb** — jump **Adjective** — cute **Adverb** — slowly	• Many children have had lots of input about **nouns**, **verbs**, **adjectives** and **adverbs** and are still confused. If this is the case, then the best option is to start the teaching process again but introduce them one by one. • Colour coding systems such as 'Colourful Semantics' (Bryan, 1997) or Shape Coding (Ebbels, 2007) provide extra information, particularly at the early stages of learning or for children who struggle with the concept. • Introduce one term at a time (see not teaching opposites together, page 155). Focus on **nouns** first. Once all can identify concrete **nouns** easily, then introduce **verbs**. Again, over-teach and do not move on too quickly. Teach these terms specifically one at a time. Similarly introduce adjectives and **adverbs** one at a time.

		• As each term is introduced provide many concrete examples with picture or object support. Then provide opportunities to sort the new term versus non-examples. e.g.: 'These are **verbs**, and these are not **verbs**.' Then look at wider applications such as underlining just one part of speech in a text. • Once a term is well-established it can then be contrasted with other parts of speech. e.g.: sort these words into **nouns**, **verbs** and **adjectives**. • These skills need to be automatic, so will take lots of revisiting. Going slow at the start, will prevent confusion later on.
1 & 2	Is aware of dictionaries, thesauri, glossaries and Word Walls.	• Play 'Dictionary definitions' game (page 127) • Provide a wide variety of dictionaries, thesauri, glossaries. Find versions that are accessible to younger word learners e.g. Collins COBUILD dictionaries are a great range of dictionaries, *Storyteller's Illustrated Dictionary* (Mrs Wordsmith, 2019). • Play Word Wall games (page 182) to increase awareness.
2	Able to use dictionaries, thesauri, glossaries and Word Walls.	• Teach dictionary skills in a structured manner ensuring students are able to find words but also apply the definitions. • Encourage access to a wide range of tools including thesauri and glossaries, paper-based tools as well as online tools. • Encourage independent use of Word Walls and Word mats (page 182).

Level 1 & 2	Understands that words have multiple meanings.
	
	Homonyms: words that sound the same are spelt the same but have different meanings
	
	Homophones: words that sound the same but are spelt differently and have different meanings.
		• Level 1: Discuss homonyms. Get children to talk about or draw different meanings of homonyms. Use the words on 'Homonyms' worksheets but do as a spoken or drawing task.
		• Level 2: Homonyms, Homophones, Heteronyms
		  ○ Introduce homonyms first and give examples.
		  ○ Then present words with multiple meanings and encourage students to give at least two meanings. As a rule, the more common the word, the more different meanings.

	Heteronyms: words that are pronounced differently, spelt the same but have different meanings.	o Use 'Do you get it?' worksheet on page 285 to analyse homonym-based jokes. o Children can draw the different meanings of the words. Compare and discuss. o Practise using the word in two (or more) different sentences, each one reflecting the different meanings. o In groups, set the task of acting out each meaning. o Use the worksheets on pages 282–284. • Level 2: Look through a text and select words which have multiple meanings. Match the meaning to the word.
1 & 2	Able to define known words clearly.	• Level 1: Start practising defining common nouns. Use the 'What am I?' prompt sheet on page 286. One person looks at a picture or object, then uses the prompts to give clues for others to guess. • Level 2: Start with familiar objects or pictures, before moving onto verbs, adjectives and more abstract nouns. See the 'Teacher notes: Teaching definitions' sheet on page 287 for guidance.
1 & 2	Able to articulate own word learning strategies.	• Level 1 & 2: Encourage children to reflect on their own strategies. • Level 2: Use 'I have skills to learn about words' page 295.

Continue to develop these skills

- Continue direct teaching of vocabulary, as this will reinforce these skills.
- Continue to structure definition skills.
- Encourage children to articulate how they independently learnt words.

Teaching Notes:
Teaching Prefixes, Suffixes and Root Words

Background knowledge for teachers

Morphemes are the smallest units of meaning within a word. For instance: 'understatement' is made up of three morphemes under + state + ment.

Bound morphemes: can only be used as part of a word, such as 'dis' in 'disinterested'.

Unbound morphemes: can exist on their own, such as 'fortune' in 'unfortunate'.

Spelling changes: words that do not have spelling changes when they are broken into morphemes such as 'appear' in 'disappear' or 'decide' in 'undecided' will develop earlier than morphemes that have spelling changes such as 'silly' to 'silliness' or 'repeat' to 'repetition'.

The following provides an overview of the general developmental process which needs to be taken into account.

Level 1 (up to 7 years): Compound words. Compound words are the starting point as they are easier for children to spot and the 'small words' both carry obvious meaning. The two words within 'snowball' may be identified as 'snow and 'ball' but also it is possible to combine words to make compound words. e.g.: 'bed' + 'time' = 'bedtime'.

To emphasise the change in meaning, draw pictures of the two 'small words' as well as the combined compound word e.g. a picture of 'snow, a ball and a snowball.'

airport	bathroom	daydream	football
jellyfish	lipstick	outdoors	everything
snowball	thunderstorm	underwear	bedtime
earache	footpath	handwriting	keyboard
playground	roundabout	shopkeeper	sunglasses
watermelon	grandmother	seaside	downstairs
toothpaste	motorbike	sunflower	grasshopper

(From list at www.firstschoolyears.com)
Use compound words activity on page 273.

Level 1 (up to 7 years): Look at how word endings affect the meaning of the word.

Talk about how simple word endings affect the meaning of the word. Write a selection of words on the board. What happens to the meaning when you add '-ed', '-ing', '-s' to a range of common verbs and nouns e.g. walk/walks/walking, cat/cats.

Level 2 (aged 7+): Introduce the terms 'prefix', 'suffix' and 'root word' one at a time. 'Prefix' may be the best place to start followed by 'suffix' and then 'root word' because prefixes have the most noticeable impact on meaning and initially 'root word' may initially be referred to as 'the word'. Introducing one term at a time will ensure they do not end up in a muddle. Even if it is counter-intuitive at this point, your colleagues who teach your class in years to come will truly thank you.

Prefix. Introduce the term 'prefix'. Start with the most common prefix which is 'un' and compare familiar words with and without 'un', e.g.: 'unfair, untrue, undone'. Ask children to think of other words and form a collection over time. Compare to non-examples such as 'uncle'. Use the list of common prefixes on page 274 as a guide. Each time select a range of familiar words and discuss how the prefix changes the word. A worksheet is on page 276.

Suffix. Once children are confident with 'prefix', introduce the term 'suffix'. Using the list on page 275 as a guide, go through the common suffixes in turn, and discuss how the addition of a suffix changes the word. Start with transparent morphemes that do not have spelling changes to start with. A worksheet is on page 277.

Root word. What is most commonly referred to as 'root word' is more accurately known as 'base word', but whichever term you use, be consistent. In this book 'root word' is used as it is more commonly used in schools.

Find words that have root words and those which do not and talk about differences. A worksheet is on page 278.

Building words. Start with a simple root word such as 'do' and brainstorm words that contain the root word, such as 'undo', 'redo', 'doing', 'undoing', 'undoable', 'done' and 'does'. Discuss how the meaning is changed by the addition of prefixes at the beginning of the word or suffixes at the end. Non-examples (words which contain the spelling of the root word but have no meaning link to it), such as 'door', will need to be discussed but its reason for rejection made clear.

At this point the 'word builder bon bon' on page 279 can be introduced, and children may take the words and break them into their component morphemes.

Examples of simple root words and their variations which can be used to practise early morphological skills with the 'word builder bon bon' on page 279.

Root word	Generated words	Non-examples
do	undo, redo, doing, undoing, undoable, done, does	door
cut	uncut, cuts, cutting	cute
catch	catches, catchy, catchiest, catchier	
sleep	sleepy, sleepless, sleepier, sleeps, asleep	
make	unmake, remake, making, maker	
dress	dresses, undress, dresser, dressed, dressing, dressmaker, dressy	
move	remove, unmoved, moves, moved, moving, movement, mover, moveable	
run	runner, rerun, runs, running, runaway, rundown, runabout	runt
motor	motors, motored, motoring, motorbike, motorcycle, motorboat, motorcade, motorcar, motorist	
walk	walks, walked, walking, sleepwalk, walkabout, walkie-talkie, walkout, walkover, walkway	
side	beside, sideboard, sideburns, sidecar, sidekick, sidelight, sideline, sideshow, sidestep, sidestroke, sidewalk, sidetrack, sideways	
after	afterwards, afterglow, after-effect, afterlife, aftermath, afternoon, aftershave, afterthought, aftershock, aftercare, afterbirth	rafter
case	suitcase, casebook, casework, cases, cased, briefcase	
ball	basketball, football, softball, ballpark, ballroom, ballpoint	

Application of morphological skills. Identify prefix, suffix and root word in a range of words. Start with structured introduction of words that require no spelling changes before moving onto words in which the root word changes spelling before eventually using incidental words that are encountered. Talk about the prefixes and suffixes and how they change the words' meanings.

Curriculum-related words that can be broken into morphological units without spelling changes include: **overlook, preventable, heroic, urbanisation, planetary, faultless, ecosystem, microscope, globalisation, epicentre, antisocial, coexist, hexagonal and inadequate.**

Curriculum related words with spelling changes: **theatrical, skeletal, intolerance, manufacturing, condensation, carnivorous, asymmetrical, picturesque, twentieth, variation, multiplication, rectangular, pollution and spherical.**

Greek and Latin roots. Greek and Latin roots become increasingly important as children move from primary/elementary school into secondary/high school. A list of the most common Greek and Latin roots and some example words are provided on page 280. Introduce the concept of etymology and how words containing the same roots are related. Compare related words and then look for more. The links are not always obvious; for instance the root 'ped' meaning foot is in both 'pedal' and 'pedestal'. *Oxford School Dictionary of Word Origins* (Ayto, 2009) is a fun introduction to etymology. The website etymonline.com is very useful for research. In-depth work may be completed in small groups. Keep an eye out for Greek and Latin roots, particularly in science and maths, where they are more common.

Level 1

Compound Words

Cut out these words. Mix them up. Match two words together to make a new word. Full size version available in the online resources which accompany this book.

bath	room
foot	ball
sun	glasses
jelly	fish
lip	stick
key	ring
down	stairs
motor	bike
round	about
water	melon
tooth	ache
play	ground
snow	ball

From list at www.firstschoolyears.com

Level 2

Prefix

misunderstanding

The Most Important Prefixes to Learn

Rank	Prefix	Meaning	Percentage of all prefixes	Examples	Non-examples
1	un-	not	26	unfair, undo, undecided, unthinkable	uncle, under, unison
2	re-	again	14	restart, reboot, redo, rewrite, recreate	remain, reason, reading, restaurant
3	in-, im-, il-, ir-	not	11	inedible, impossible, illegible, illegal, irrelevant	ink, internet, imperial, Ilford, Irish, iron
4	dis-	not	7	disappear, disband	dish, distance, discus
5	non-	not	4	non-smoker, nonsense, non-disposable	none
6	in-	in, within	4	inbred, income	inch, ink
7	mis-	wrongly	3	mislead, misjudge	misty, miss
Total			69%		

Adapted from White et al., 2009

Level 2

Suffix

misunderstand**ing**

The Most Important Suffixes to Learn

Rank	Suffix	Meaning	Percentage of all suffixes	Examples	Non-examples
1	-s, -es	More than one or marks present tense	31	cats, fishes, runs, hops	miss, this
2	-ed	Marks past tense	20	walked, slammed	bed, red
3	-ing	Marks present tense	14	eating, singing	ring, thing
4	-ly	Adverb	7	slowly, fiercely	sly, fly
5	-er, –or (agent)	Person who does verb	4	teacher, actor, singer, dictator, footballer	for, beer
6	-ion, -tion, -ation	Makes a word into a noun e.g. 'dictate' is a verb but 'dictation' is a noun.	4	dictation, emotion, repetition, circulation, immigration	potion, lotion
Total			80%		

Adapted from White et al., 2009

Level 2

Prefix

misunderstanding

Name .... Date ....

How do Prefixes Change a Word?

Look at the pairs of words below. Circle the prefix. Write how the prefix changes the meaning of the word. The first one is done for you. If you don't know what a word means you can ask a friend or look it up in a dictionary.

No prefix	With prefix	How does the prefix change the word
fair	unfair	The 'un' makes something that is fair and good into something that is bad.
start	restart	
appear	disappear	
sense	nonsense	
do	undo	
write	rewrite	
possible	impossible	
stuck	unstuck	
polite	impolite	
formal	informal	
connect	disconnect	

Level 2

Suffix

Name .... Date ....

How do Suffixes Change a Word?

Look at the pairs of words below. Circle the suffix. Write how the suffix changes the meaning of the word. The first one is done for you. If you don't know what a word means you can ask a friend or look it up in a dictionary.

No suffix	With suffix	How does the suffix change the word
dog	dog(s)	Adding the 's' means there is more than one dog.
football	footballer	
cry	crying	
glass	glasses	
visit	visiting	
jump	jumped	
quick	quickly	
visit	visitor	
crush	crushed	
odd	oddly	

Level 2

Root

mis**understand**ing

Name .... **Date** ....

Find the Root Word

Look at the list of words below. Write the root word in the second column. Write the prefix and suffix in the last column. The first one is done for you.

Word	Write the root word	Write the prefix and / or suffix
acting	*act*	*ing*
dislike		
running		
quickly		
teacher		
impatient		
unlikable		
impossibly		
reassuring		
disappearance		

Level 2

Prefix

misunderstanding

Root

mis**understand**ing

Suffix

misunderstand**ing**

Word Builder Bon Bon
Prefix, Root and Suffix

Name .... Date ....

Look at the sweet wrappers below. The root word is written on the sweet. On the first one you can see that the possible prefixes are written on the left-hand 'wrapper' and suffixes added on the right-hand side. Fill in the prefixes and suffixes for the other words. Options are given below.

Prefixes (at the beginning)	Suffixes (at the end)
dis, out, re, un	able, ed, ful, ing, less, ment, s

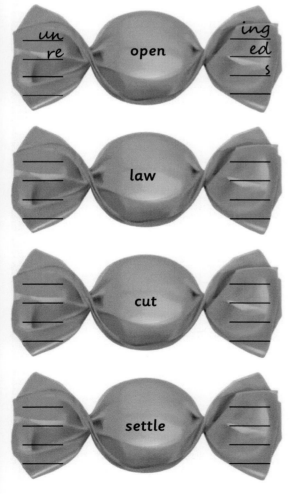

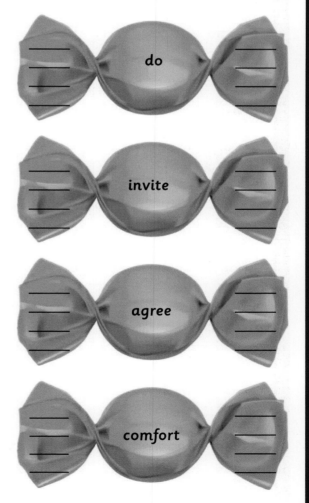

Level 2

Root

misunderstanding

Greek and Latin Root Words

Root	Meaning	Origin	Examples
aud	hearing	Latin	audio, audition, auditorium
auto	self	Greek	autograph, autobiography, automatic, automated
astro	star	Greek	astronomy, astrology, astronaut, asterisk
bio	life	Greek	biography, biology, autobiography, bionic, antibiotic
dic, dict	speak, tell	Latin	dictation, dictator, verdict, predict, contradict
graph	to write, to draw	Greek	autograph, biography, photograph, telegraph
ject	throw	Latin	reject, deject, project, inject, projection
logos, logy	study	Greek	geology, astrology, biology, technology, psychology, mythology
meter	measure	Greek	meter, thermometer, centimetre, symmetry
micro	small	Greek	microscopic, microscope, microwave, microbe
min	small, little	Latin	minimal, minimize, minimum, mini, miniature, minuscule, minute, minority
mit, mis	send	Latin	mission, transmit, missile, submission, permit, emit

path	feeling, suffering	Greek	pathetic, sympathy, empathy
ped	foot	Latin	pedestrian, pedal, pedicure, pedestal
port	carry	Latin	port, transport, transportation, portable
rupt	to break	Latin	disrupt, interrupt, rupture, corrupt
script	to write	Latin	scribble, manuscript, prescription
scope	look at	Greek	microscope, telescope, kaleidoscope
spect	see	Latin	respect, inspection, inspector, spectator, spectacles
sol	sun	Latin	solar, solar system, parasol
struct	build, form	Latin	instruct, construction, destruct, instrument
tele	distant	Greek	telephone, television, telegraph, telescope

https://www.academia.edu/31390651/Common_Prefixes_Suffixes_and_Roots_The_20_Most_Common_Prefixes_in_Academic_Texts

Level 2

Homonyms: Words that Sound the Same, Have the Same Spelling but Have Different Meanings

Name .... **Date** ....

Write down two meanings of each word. Draw small pictures if you prefer.

Words	Meaning 1	Meaning 2
bat	Small flying animal	Used to play sports
letter		
key		
light		
street		
can		
sign		
park		
back		

Level 2

Name .... Date ....

Homophones: Words that Sound the Same but are Spelt Differently and Have Different Meanings

Say each word out loud. Notice how each pair of words sounds the same but is spelt differently. Write a meaning for each word. Draw small pictures to show the meaning if you prefer.

Word	Meaning	Word that sounds the same	Meaning
blew	*past tense of blow*	blue	*colour*
board		bored	
knot		not	
hear		here	
hole		whole	
guessed		guest	
flour		flower	
knight		night	

Copyright material from Stephen Parsons and Anna Branagan (2022), *Word Aware 1*, Routledge

Level 2

Name .... **Date** ....

Heteronyms: Words that are Pronounced Differently, Spelt the Same but have Different Meanings

Write down two meanings of each word. Draw small pictures if you prefer. Say the words out loud, to check you know how.

Words	Meaning 1	Meaning 2
lead	To be ahead of others	A metal
contest		
desert		
excuse		
minute		
object		
permit		
refuse		
row		
tear		

Level 2

Name: .... **Date:** ....

Do You Get It?

These jokes are funny because some words have two meanings. Can you write the two different meanings of the highlighted words? The first one is done for you.

	Meaning 1	Meaning 2
Q: Why is a football stadium so cool? A: Because it is full of **fans**.	A football supporter	Something that keeps you cool
Q: What did the traffic light say to the car? A: Don't look now, I'm **changing**.		
Q: Why are chefs so cruel? A: Because they **beat** eggs.		
Q: Why is the sea friendly? A: Because it is giving little **waves**.		
Q: What is a witch's favourite subject in school? A: **Spelling.**		
Q: What kind of tree fits in your hand? A: A **palm** tree.		
Q: Why did the cookie go to the hospital? A: Because he felt **crummy**.		
Q: How do you get a squirrel to like you? A: Act like a **nut**!		

(Anderson, 1998) https://redtri.com/best-jokes-for-kids/slide/3

What am I?

- You find me . . .

- I can . . .

- An important thing about me is . . .

- When you look at me, you can see . . .

Example: 'You find me in the kitchen. I can cook food. An important thing about me is that I get hot. When you look at me, you can see a handle and lid. I am a . . .'

Level 2

Teaching Notes:
Teaching Definition Skills

Some words are much easier to define that others. In general:

| Concrete nouns (things that can be touched and seen) | adjectives | verbs | abstract nouns (e.g.: concepts such as 'responsibility' or 'civilisation') |

Easiest to define　　　　　　　　　　　　　　　　　　　　　　Hardest to define

The steps outlined below provide a structure to support children to develop definitional skills, which are a high-level language task, and will take a number of years to fully develop. At each step ensure skills are applied to a wide range of words. The words should be familiar to the children because the aim is to teach definition skills as opposed to new words, and this is best done when children have lots of knowledge to draw upon. A list of words is provided on pages 291 to 294. If using other words, check that the process is easy to apply, and in particular that any abstract words have simpler synonyms.

Steps for defining words

Step 1: think about what you know about the word

Start with concrete nouns and encourage children to talk about what the object can be used for, who in particular might use it and its category. Once children are confident with concrete nouns, move onto adjectives and then verbs, before abstract nouns.

Discussion points may be recorded on a mind map. The following 'Getting started with defining words' is available to copy on page 290.

- Concrete nouns:　　　　　　　what can it do?/what can it be used for?

　　　　　　　　　　　　　　　　　It is a kind of . . . (category)

- Adjectives:　　　　　　　　　It can be used to describe . . . and . . .

- Verbs:　　　　　　　　　　　　Who or what does this?

- Abstract nouns:　　　　　　　This word has something to do with . . .

Step 2: compare it to a word you know

This is a crucial word learning skill and will require application to a wide number of words.

Encourage children to think of a simple synonym. Compare the target word and the synonym:

- 'How are they the same and different?'
- Identify the specific applications of the word by asking 'What is special about the new word?' and 'When is it particularly good to use this word?'

Use the 'Synonym Venn Diagram' (page 229) to record.

Step 3: define the word

This step is only possible when the preceding steps are well established.

From what has been discussed, highlight the most relevant information. Select a sentence starter and prompt children to define the word. Check that the definition cannot be easily confused with other words.

- (This word) is something that can . . .
- (This word) is someone who can . . .
- (This word) is a kind of . . .
- (This word) is used . . .
- Someone who is described as (this word) . . .
- Something that is described as (this word) is . . .
- (This word) is something that. . . . can do when . . .
- (This word) is like . . . but . . .

The 'Word Wall definition clues' on page 185 may be used as prompts.

Step 4: check the definition

This can follow on immediately after 'Step 3'.

- Compare the definition with the dictionary. It is OK if they are a bit different, but make sure the dictionary's meaning is captured in your definition.
- Children working independently can check their definition with another child. Are others able to guess when they read their definition? What information do they need to add to make it better?

Promoting independence

Start with higher levels of support and reduce this as children master the task and become more independent.

- High support activities:
  - o discuss what children know about the word and write this on the board
  - o select the sentence starter in Step 3 or the 'Word Wall definition clues' (page 185)
  - o model responses.
- Intermediate support:
  - o Children work in pairs
  - o Provide 'Getting started with defining words' (see page 290), 'Synonym Venn diagram' (page 229) and 'Word Wall definition clues' (page 185).
- Independent:
  - o Children write definitions of words they know well. Self-check against definitions in the COBUILD Primary Learner's Dictionary (2018).

Continued opportunities to develop definition skills

- Use the Word Wall definition clues.
- Define words from the Word Wall or Word Pot which are relatively new to them.
- Define words for peers in a way that is helpful.

Example

Responsibility

This is an abstract noun, so would not be tackled until children were able to define concrete nouns, verbs and adjectives.

Step 1: Encourage contributions about '**responsibility**'. They can be quite broad at this point. Information added to the mind map may include: owning up, being honest, playing your part, being sensible, being reliable and your job to do it. Highlight the contributions which are most helpful, perhaps in this case 'sensible' and 'reliable'.

Step 2: Use the 'Synonym Venn diagram' (page 229) and compare the word to a synonym. In this case the best synonym may be 'sensible,' as it is the word which children are most familiar with. Discuss how '**responsibility**' and 'sensible' are the same and different.

Step 3: Choose a sentence starter. The most flexible one for abstract nouns is '(This word) is like . . . but . . .' For this example: '**Responsibility** is a bit like being sensible, because they are both helpful ways to behave, but with **responsibility** sometimes you might need to step up and be in charge or say when you are wrong.'

Getting Started with Defining Words

1 For **concrete nouns**, which are things you can touch and see.

Think about:

what can it do?/what can it be used for?

It is a kind of . . . (category)

2 For **adjectives**, which describe things. Think about two different things it can describe.

It can be used to describe . . . and . . .

3 **Verbs**. Think in particular who or what does this action. Don't just say 'people'. Name the type of person or when.

Who or what does this?

4 **Abstract nouns** label things which are ideas. They are not always things you can see.

'Health' and 'success' are abstract nouns. They are hard to define but start off with thinking of what it is to do with.

This word has something to do with . . .

Level 2

Words to Practise Definition Skills

A full size version of this resource is available in the online resources which accompany this book. See page i for details on how to access.

Concrete nouns

compass	litter	elbow
suitcase	toad	computer
magazine	moon	waterfall
flea	triangle	lettuce
gravy	office	earth
marshmallow	professor	postcard

Adjectives

mysterious	afraid	gigantic
splendid	hollow	scarlet
elegant	bitter	dependable
confused	clumsy	bruised
dull	bossy	scruffy
remarkable	invisible	heroic

Verbs

creep	howl	nibble
concentrate	search	hatch
shiver	tug	twinkle
browse	create	greet
tumble	drown	slash
organise	study	dive

Abstract nouns

fashion	wisdom	beginning
crisis	power	grudge
responsibility	discovery	success
determination	memory	risk
forgiveness	health	attitude
communication	permission	explanation

Level 2

Name: .... **Date:** ....

I Have Skills to Learn About Words

1. I can define words that I know. Here's a word and its definition:

   Word:

   Definition:

2. I know what prefixes and suffixes are.

   Prefix

   Here's a word with a prefix:

   Suffix

   Here's a word with a suffix:

3. I can look out for words within words. Here's one I found:

4. I know that words are on our Word Wall and in our class Word Pot.

   A word on the Word Wall is . . .

   A word in the Word Pot is . . .

5. I know that words can have more than one meaning

   Here's a word with two meanings, and this is what it means.

   1

   2

6. I know how to look words up in dictionaries. Here's a word I looked up in the dictionary to find out more about it.

4. We Know What to Do to Try and Work Out What a Word Means

Level	Skill	Activities
1 & 2	When reading or sharing a text, applies background, picture or text knowledge to work out a word's meanings. (Note: We are not focussing on decoding here, we are focussing on words that children do not understand.)	• Model the process. Activate prior knowledge by discussing general themes and context. Stop, identify a word that the children may not know and talk through hypotheses. Start with made-up words or blanked out words (cloze procedure).
2	Spontaneously re-reads sections of text to work out a word's meaning.	• Replace words in paragraphs with either made-up words or blanks (cloze procedure), independently children try and work out what the word is. Beck et al., (2002) highlight that many contexts are less than helpful and may even be mis-directive, so start with helpful practice examples. • Model the process. • Introduce the 'Stop' bookmark on page 298 as a reminder.
2	Spontaneously able to identify part of speech (e.g. noun) and looks within words (e.g. prefixes) to work out a its meaning.	• Model identifying an unknown word's part of speech • Made up words or blanked words can be used for students' practising. • Model and practise analysing word affixes to work out word meanings in whole class and small group activities.
1 & 2	Able to talk through strategies used to work out what words mean.	• Level 1 & 2: Encourage children to talk through their problem solving. • Level 2: Model the whole process as outlined in the 'I can work out what words mean by myself' worksheet on page 299. • Level 2: Encourage children to complete the worksheet independently.

Continue to develop these skills

- Level 1 & 2: Model using contextual clues to work out meaning during whole class or small group reading.

- Level 2: Ensure students use the 'Stop' bookmarks as reminders.

- Students complete the 'I can work out what words mean by myself' worksheet on page 299 from time to time.

- Level 2: After independent reading children feed back words they have worked out the meaning of and how they did it.

Level 2

Stop bookmarks

Used to help students just stop and reflect about what a new word means.

When you are reading, and it does not make sense	When you are reading, and it does not make sense	When you are reading, and it does not make sense
STOP	STOP	STOP
Re-read the sentence.	Re-read the sentence.	Re-read the sentence.
Re-read the paragraph.	Re-read the paragraph.	Re-read the paragraph.
Think for a moment about what you know already.	Think for a moment about what you know already.	Think for a moment about what you know already.
Try and work it out.	Try and work it out.	Try and work it out.
If you're still not sure, then look it up in a dictionary or ask someone.	If you're still not sure, then look it up in a dictionary or ask someone.	If you're still not sure, then look it up in a dictionary or ask someone.
Check if what you have learnt now makes sense.	Check if what you have learnt now makes sense.	Check if what you have learnt now makes sense.

Level 2

Name: .... Date: ....

I Can Work Out What Words Mean by Myself

Read and think	The book I was reading	
	The page I stopped on because I did not understand a word	
	The new word I found	
	The sentence it was in	
Part of speech Noun — ball Verb — jump Adjective — cute Adverb — slowly	The word's part of speech. e.g.: noun or verb.	
Prefix — **mis**understanding Suffix — misunderstand**ing**	The word's prefix, suffix and root (if it has any).	
Read and think	I read the paragraph the word was in and a little bit before. The background information that helped me . . .	
	I think the new word means . . .	
Check it makes sense by talking through the paragraph in your own words but including the new word.		

5. We Find Out About New Words

Level	Skill	Activities
1 & 2	Will ask someone if they don't know what a word means.	• Model the strategy. • Put in place 'word buddies' to children to ask each other. • Tell families of the strategy and get them involved. • Display the poster on page 301.
2	Independently uses dictionaries, thesauri and glossaries to look up words (paper-form or on-line)	• Make an information station: word learning resources can all be collated into a small area as suggested by Graves and Watts-Taffe (2009). • Teach skills specifically including alphabetical listings, understanding the meaning and checking it makes sense. • Display the poster on page 302. • Send home 'homework for families' (page 303) so families can model how to look up words.
2	When words have multiple meanings, able to select the appropriate definition for a word.	• Practise using the worksheets 'choosing the right homonym' and 'choosing the right heteronym' on pages 305–306. • Model further examples.
2	Now have a complete set of independent word learning skills	• Use the bookmark on page 307.

Continue to develop these skills

- Ensure dictionaries and thesauri are available.
- Retain strategies such as 'word buddies', bookmarks and posters.
- Continue to model how to choose an appropriate definition for multiple-meaning words.

 If I don't know a word, I can ask someone.

I can ask a child, an adult or someone at home.

 **If I come across a word I don't know...**

I can ask someone or look it up.

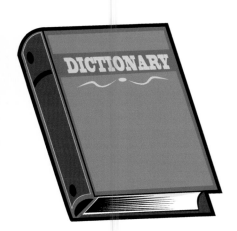 

Look in a dictionary, thesaurus or glossary.

Level 2

Name .... Date ....

Homework for Families

Your child is a great word learner. At school they have been learning lots of new words. Part of being a good word learner is being a good 'word detective'. This involves trying to work out what a word means by themselves, looking up words in a dictionary or asking other people.

Your child's teacher has given them this list of words. To help your child learn new words they have been asked to talk to you about what the words mean. The idea is that you tell your child what you know about each word. Try to use simple words to explain what a word means. If you are unsure about what a word means, look it up together either in a dictionary or online. It all helps with the learning process.

New words	Who helped	Definitions

Level 2

Name .... Date ....

Homework for Parents who Write More than One Language

Please translate these words into your home language and talk about what they mean. It will help your child learn new words. Talking about the words is the important part.

New words (in English)	Translation (in home language)

Level 2

Name .... **Date** ....

Choosing the Right Homonym

Homonym: words that sound the same and are spelt the same but have different meanings.

Circle the meaning which matches the word's meaning in the sentence. Tell someone how you worked it out.

1. Deep in the cave I heard something moving and wondered if it was a **bat**.		
bat	(Flying mammal)	Used to play sports.
2. I listened out all day as I was expecting an important **letter**.		
letter	a, b, c . . .	It can be posted.
3. The **key** was faded and so it was hard to work out exactly where we were.		
key	Object to unlock a door.	Guide to features on a map.
4. I was quite happy to pick up the lamps as I knew they were **light**.		
light	Not heavy.	Provides illumination.
5. The manager was very happy to see his new striker **sign** the contract.		
sign	To tell you where to go.	To write your name.
6. Mum was going to be late for her exercise class as she could not find a **park**.		
park	A place with trees and grass.	What you do with a car.

Level 2

Name: .... **Date:** ....

Choosing the Right Heteronym

Heteronym: words that sound different but are spelt the same and have different meanings.

Circle the meaning which matches the word's meaning in the sentence. Tell someone how you worked it out, and check that you say it right too.

1. Marina offered to take the **lead** as Florence had a terrible sense of direction.		
Lead	(To be ahead of others.)	A soft metal.
2. Iqbal was keen to enter the **contest** as he thought he was good at throwing.		
Contest	To argue.	A match of skill.
3. Whoever thought that an insect so **minute** could cause so much pain?		
Minute	60 seconds.	Tiny.
4. The bin collectors will **refuse** to take the recycling if it contains any broken glass.		
Refuse	To deny.	Rubbish/garbage.
5. 'Listen up, I need you all to sit in a **row**!' our teacher shouted.		
Row	A line.	An argument.
6. One **tear** dropped to the floor as he looked at the torn picture.		
Tear	When you cry.	To rip paper.

Level 2

'What Does that Word Mean?' Bookmarks

Use to help children work out what a word means.

6. We Remember and Use New Words

Level	Skill	Activities
1 & 2	Uses words that have been learnt spontaneously when writing and speaking.	Use one or a combination of: • Level 1 & 2: Encouraging children to listen out for when their new word is used. • Level 1 & 2: Talk to teacher, peer or family member about the new words they have learnt. • Level 2: Children record when they use a word in their personal dictionary. See page 309. • Level 2: Write words in the personal dictionary in sentences.
2	Has a method for recording new words they want to remember.	Use one or a combination of: • Personal dictionary: in a small notebook write new words and a little about them or complete sheets similar to the one on page 309 and make them into a booklet. • Write words on 'Post-it' notes as they read. • 'Word Collector' bookmark see page 92. • Complete a 'Word Wizard' independently.

Continue to develop these skills

• Level 1 & 2: From time to time have peer to peer and class discussions about words they have learnt.

• Level 1 & 2: Set a task for children to use their new words in sentences.

• Level 2: Keep going with the chosen recording method, e.g.: personal dictionary, 'Post-it' notes, 'Word Wizard' or bookmarks.

• Level 2: In their own written work, children highlight words they have recently learnt.

Level 2

Personal Dictionary

Name: .... Date: ....

New word

I found my new word in . . .

I can say it. I can spell it.

I can explain it in my own words here . . .

I can write it in a sentence here . . .

This word is useful to me because . . .

Keep looking and listening out about it. Write a bit more about it when you see or hear it again. I used this word on . . . . I said or wrote . . . . .

Now this word is mine to keep!

7. We Help Other People Learn New Words

Level	Skill	Activities
1 & 2	For familiar words, able to define words in a way that is helpful to others.	• Establish a 'word buddy' system as part of the class routine. • Practise defining words by playing Word Wall or Word Pot games.
2	Able to show others how to use word learning tools such as dictionaries.	• Encourage students to tell others how they found out about a word. Compare different methods.

Continue to develop these skills

- Establish a 'word buddy' system in which children are encouraged to ask each other about word meanings.
- Set up opportunities for older children to coach children from younger classes to develop word learning strategies. For example, when reading with a younger child, encourage conversations about unknown words and looking for clues about word meaning.

References

Anderson, P. (1998). *My First Joke Book*. London: Young Corgi Books.

Ayto, J. (2009). *Oxford School Dictionary of Word Origins*. Oxford: Oxford University Press.

Beck, I., McKeown, M. & Kucan L. (2002). *Bringing Words to Life*: *Robust Vocabulary Instruction*. New York: Guilford Press.

Benelli, B., Belacchi, C., Gini, G. & Lucangeli, D. (2006). To define means to say what you know about things: The development of definitional skills as metalinguistic acquisition. *Journal of Child Language*, 33, 71–97.

Bryan, A. (1997). *Colourful semantics*. In S. Chiat, J. Law & J. Marshall (Eds.), *Language Disorders in Children and Adults: Psycholinguistic Approaches to Therapy*. London: Whurr.

Collins COBUILD Primary Learner's Dictionary (2018). Glasgow: HarperCollins.

Coxhead, A. (2000). A new academic word list. *TESOL Quarterly*, 34, 213–238.

Ebbels, S. (2007). Teaching grammar to school-aged children with specific language impairment using shape coding. *Child Language Teaching and Therapy*, 23:1, 67–93.

Ford-Connors, E. & Paratore, J. (2015). Vocabulary instruction in fifth grade and beyond: Sources of word learning and productive contexts for development. *Review of Educational Research*, 85:1, 50–91.

Graves, M. (2004). Teaching prefixes: As good as it gets? In J.F. Baumann & E.J. Kame'enui (Eds.), *Vocabulary Instruction: Research into Practice*, New York: Guilford Press.

Graves, M. & Watts-Taffe, S. (2009). For the love of words: Fostering word consciousness in young readers. In M. Graves (Ed.), *Essential Readings on Vocabulary Instruction*. Newark, DE: International Reading Association.

Levesque, K., Kieffer, M. & Deacon, S. (2019). Inferring meaning from meaningful parts: The contributions of morphological skills to the development of children's reading comprehension. *Reading Research Quarterly*, 54:1, 63–80.

Lyster, S., Lervåg, A. & Hulme, C. (2016). Preschool morphological training produces long-term improvements in reading comprehension. *Reading and Writing*, 29, 1269–1288.

Nippold, M. & Sun, L. (2008). Knowledge of morphologically complex words: A developmental study of older children and young adolescents. *Language, Speech and Hearing Services in Schools*, 39, 365–373.

Rastle, K. (2019). The place of morphology in learning to read in English. *Cortex,* 116, 45–54.

Sparks, E. & Deacon, H. (2015). Morphological awareness and vocabulary acquisition: A longitudinal examination of their relationship in English-speaking children. *Applied Psycholinguistics*, 36:2, 299–321.

White, T., Sowell J. & Yanagihara, A. (2009). Teaching elementary students to use word part clues. In M. Graves (Ed.), *Essential Readings on Vocabulary Instruction*. Newark, DE: International Reading Association.

Wordsmith, Mrs. (2019). *Storyteller's Illustrated Dictionary.* London: Mrs Wordsmith.

Families

Families

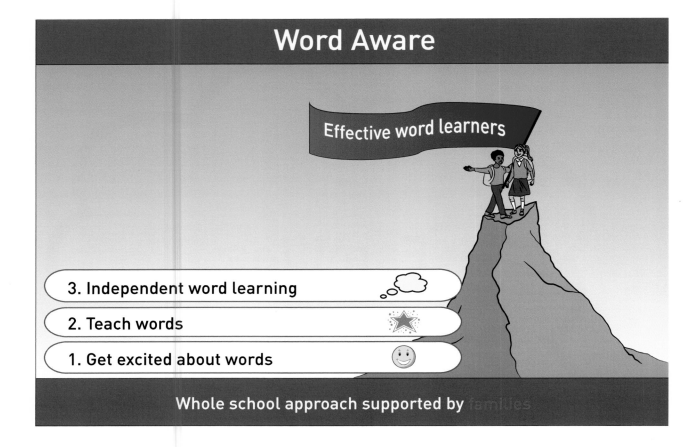

The *Word Aware* approach is a whole school approach underpinned by families. Vocabulary learning does not happen exclusively in school and so children will learn more if schools and families work together. The challenge is to engage families in a way that is meaningful, manageable and effective. We want all families to get involved, but in particular we need to engage families for whom vocabulary is not an area of interest.

As with *Word Aware* in school, the best place to start with families is to involve them in 'Get Excited About Words'. Celebrating words and playing word games are about having fun and interacting, so are less threatening to some.

Involve Families in Celebrating Words

Activities include

- Sending home the word games on pages 317–320.
- Running a family word workshop (page 35) will deepen understanding and support links with what is happening in school.
- Getting all staff and children to dress up as a favourite word. Families are invited in to watch their children and play some word games (page 37).

- Word Challenge day. All children are sent home with a word challenge on the same day (page 37).

- Word of the week. There is one word for younger children and one for older children that the whole school community gets involved with. Get families involved with the challenges that are set each week (page 39).

- Newsletter ideas for families. Regularly put ideas in the newsletter (page 80).

- Encourage parents, carers and grandparents to help out at the school events, Can they help out at the 'Winning words' tombola (page 83) or 'Digging for vocabulary treasure'? (page 86).

- Sending home 'Word collector' bookmarks (for collecting interesting words, page 92) or 'Finding different words' bookmarks (for finding different types of words, page 93).

- Finding 'Treasure chest' words. These prompt children to collect a bit more information about words they have identified (page 94).

- Instructions on how to make your own riddles or jokes are on page 102. These come with a health warning: they are very bad jokes but will provide families with lots of word fun.

- 'My favourite word.' Encourage family members to send in photos of themselves holding their favourite word poster or their favourite word written on piece of paper (page 114).

- Involve families in craft activities (see page 118).

Send Home Information on Accessing Audiobooks

Reading supports vocabulary development, so any school initiative which supports reading will also support vocabulary. Encourage families to read to their children more challenging books than children can read. In addition, encourage families to access audiobooks. Send home 'Helping your child to learn words: listen to stories' (page 321).

Key Information to Share with Families

The key messages for parents are given as a handout on page 322 for families comfortable with written information. Other parents may need this information more verbally. Families who speak a language other than English, may need information verbally or translated. **It is really important that families discuss words in a language they are fluent in.** This needs to be the unequivocal message from all school staff.

The key messages for all families which may need repeating in various formats:

- Learning words is really important. The more words your child knows, the more it will help them at school.

- When families help children to learn words, it really makes a difference.

- It is about talking as much as reading and writing, so talk about words.

- If your child comes home with a word from school or you find a new word in a book, tell them more about the word. Try not to ask them too many questions. Instead show them how you use the word.

- If you do not know a word, look it up on your phone or in a dictionary. That way you are showing them how to learn more.

- Encourage reading for the fun of it. Read to your child, take them to libraries, find books or magazines about things that interest them, or listen to audiobooks.
- If you speak another language at home, talk about words in the language you are most confident in.
- Have fun and join in!

Helping your child learn words: Play word games

Word games are a great way to get your child interested in words. The more words we know the easier it is to get on in life. We learn best when we are having fun. Play word games when you are travelling somewhere: walking home, in cars, on buses or trains. You just need to have learnt a couple of games, so you are ready to play at any time. The first few games are the easiest.

I went shopping

This game is good for developing memory, so is good for adults too. One person starts by saying, 'I went shopping and I bought a . . .' (names a food item). The second player says, 'I went shopping and I bought . . .' and repeats the first player's item before adding their own. The third player continues, saying the first two items before adding their own. And so on. See how many you can remember. A variation of this game is: 'I went on holiday and I packed . . .'

What am I?

For younger children, riddles need to be straightforward, rather than the conundrums that older children enjoy so much. Three to four simple clues are usually adequate, for example:

- You find me . . .
- I can . . .
- An important thing about me is . . .
- When you look at me, you can see . . .

Example: 'You find me in the kitchen. I can cook food. An important thing about me is that I get hot. When you look at me, you can see a handle and lid. I am a . . .'

I spy

Play the traditional 'I spy' game. 'I spy with my little eye something beginning with . . . (letter)'.

Variation 1: Thinking hat. Word meaning clues are given rather than letters and the object does not need to be within sight. Say, 'I put on my thinking hat and think of something that is (give a clue).' If incorrect say, 'It's not that. I put on my thinking hat and think of something that is (original clue and a second clue).' Continue until the word has been guessed. E.g.: 'I put on my thinking hat and think of something that is spicy.'

Variation 2: Big brain. In this game players give a clue containing the first sound of the word as well as a word meaning clue. Unlike 'I spy', players do not need to be able to see the item, but they

need to think with their 'big brains'. For example, 'I think with my big brain, something that is part of a tree and begins with a "b." '

Word rounds

Choose one of the categories below. Go around the circle, with each player adding a category item.

Variation: After you have chosen your category set a timer for one minute. Taking turns around the group see how many words can be generated in one minute. Record the family total and then try to beat it next time.

Easier

Animals	Clothes	Food
Things you can see at the seaside	Things you would see at the zoo	Boys'/girls' names
Transport	Things in a classroom	Verbs (things we can do e.g. jump, walk, swim)

Harder

Things you can cut	Things you can smell	Toys and games
Somewhere you go on holiday	Countries	Adjectives (describing words e.g. long, pink, smelly)
Things that are cold	Things with legs	Sports
Things that grow	Books	Emotions
Things that are fast	Things that are red	Things that open
Furniture	Living things	Things that make noise
Shops	Breakable objects	Things that are long

What can it do?

Pick one of the words below. Can you think of five things that it can do or that can be done with it? For example, **tree**: climb, chop, grow, fall down and absorb carbon dioxide.

apple	baby	ball	bread	chalk
giraffe	leaf	lion	lollipop stick	paper
paperclip	pencil	penguin	rubber band	stick
tree	your foot	your hand	cat	flour
flower	hair	water	air	spoon

Alison is an acrobat in Asia

Start at the beginning of the alphabet the first player must generate a name, profession and place that all begin with that letter. For example, for the letter 'a': 'Alison is an acrobat in Asia'. The next player then has to do the letter 'b': 'Bob is a builder in Benidorm'. Make it more complex and add adjectives, so it becomes 'Alison is an ambitious acrobat in Asia'. To make it easier, try name, food and a place in a house e.g. 'Alison is eating apples in the attic'.

Describe it!

Take a look at www.pobble365.com and look at the amazing images. Choose a picture and talk about it in turn. Support your child by taking in turns to talk about all the things you can see, how the picture makes you feel, what might someone be thinking, what might happen next, how someone or something is moving, what might someone say or what sort of person they are. Make the picture the start of an exciting adventure story.

What's the same and what's different?

Select two related words from a topic that your child is interested in and together talk about what is the same and different about two things:

- Book or film characters, e.g. Superman and Batman, Sirius and Voldemort
- Sports, e.g. rugby and football, basketball and volleyball.

- Hobbies, e.g. different computer games, computer games and board games, reading and films
- Restaurant chains, e.g.: Nandos vs McDonalds

Don't say it!

Cut out the words below or think of your own words. They might be related to what your child has learnt at school or any words that they are familiar with. Place all the words in a 'hat'. Each person takes a turn at taking out words from the hat. The challenge is to describe the word without using the word at all.

hill	trolley	graph	desert
dinosaur	fly swat	spaceship	cornflakes
mountain	biscuit	storm	flood
tree	umbrella	bee	baby
geography	daisy	crocodile	cinema
planets	purse	moon	present
spider	earthquake	tiger	America

Word associations

One player starts by saying a word. The next player says a word that is related to the first word. It can be related in any way. If another player cannot see how the words are related, they can challenge and the connection needs to be explained. Keep going until a word is repeated or a connection cannot be explained. Here's an example: Egypt – Mummy – Dad – beard – Santa Claus – Christmas – trees – leaves – departs – trains.

20 questions

One person thinks of an object. Others try and guess what it is by asking questions. The original player can only answer yes, no or maybe. Give a clue if they are on the wrong track. Can they guess it in 20 questions?

Play word games, have fun and your child's vocabulary will grow.

Children learn words when they listen to stories

Stories are fun, but they are also a great way to learn new words, which in turn will help them in school. When listening to audiobooks and podcasts, children hear lots of new words, including harder words than they are able to read.

It's great for children to listen to audiobooks on their own but it's even better to listen to them together and share your enjoyment. Long car journeys are the perfect time to share a story. Shared earphones can also work on a train. Talk about what is happening. Stop once in a while and predict what might happen next. If you miss a bit, ask your child to explain. If you are at home, draw pictures of what you think characters and places might look like. Discuss similarities and differences. Act out exciting parts.

Choose a word that you heard in the audiobook. Talk about its meaning, write it down and stick it somewhere like the fridge. Challenge everyone in the family to use and listen out for it. At the end of the day say it in a new sentence.

Here are some options for audiobooks, but there are many more.

Borrowbox: Families can access audiobooks from libraries for free. Often you never need to even go to a library, it can all be done on-line. Download the 'Borrowbox' app to download eBooks and audiobooks. You still need your library card number and your local library needs to be signed up to the scheme.

SEN charities: There are charities that offer a good range of audiobooks for children with some additional need. You do not need to provide evidence of this need, just state what the difficulty is. These services charge.

www.calibre.org.uk

www.listening-books.org.uk

LibriVox provides free downloads of out of copyright books such as *Heidi, Black Beauty and The Adventures of Tom Sawyer.* These are read by volunteers.

www.librivox.org.uk

Helping your child learn words

- Learning words is really important. The more words your child knows, the more it will help them at school.

- When families help their children learn words, it really makes a difference.

- It's about talking as much as reading and writing, so talk about words.

- If your child comes home with a word from school or you find a new word in a book, tell them more about the word. Try not to ask them too many questions. Instead show them how you use the word.

- If you don't know a word, look it up on your phone or in a dictionary. That way you are showing them how to learn more.

- Encourage reading for the fun of it. Read to your child, take them to libraries, find books or magazines about things that interest them or listen to audiobooks.

- If you speak another language at home, talk about meaning of words in the language you are most confident in.

- Have fun and join in!

Outcomes and Evaluation

Measuring the impact of any intervention is important and we had hoped to have progressed further than we have with investigating the impact of *Word Aware*. Vocabulary teaching is worth studying because it impacts right across the curriculum, however it presents researchers with some thorny issues, such as 'How many words do you need to teach to have an impact'? and 'How do you know when a child knows a word?'

A number of researchers and practitioners have chosen to investigate *Word Aware*, and a brief summary of projects is provided below. We will continue to pursue future research and are also willing to support anyone interesting in researching *Word Aware* and are hopeful that further learning will be shared in the future. Contact us via our website, thinkingtalking.co.uk, if you seek any advice or have outcomes to share.

Study 1

City, University of London / University of Oxford: Herman et al. (2020)

A joint phonics and vocabulary approach was used to teach reading to Reception children (aged 4 to 5 years) attending mainstream schools and specialist hearing provisions. *Word Aware* was selected as the method for the direct teaching of word-meaning. The schools in the study also included high numbers of children who spoke English as an Additional Language. The restricted range of words available via the phonics scheme resulted many of the target words not meeting the 'Goldilocks' criteria. On standardised measures, children in the intervention made significant gains on word reading and on expressive language, but not on receptive language.

Study 2

West Dunbartonshire: Moran & Moir (2018)

Teachers in three nursery schools used the STAR approach to teach a small number of words selected from whole class books. Children were all aged 3 to 5 years, and the schools were in areas of high deprivation. Children's knowledge of the words was measured before and after the intervention. Their knowledge of the words increased significantly and children from all socio-economic strata progressed similarly. Parents were engaged in word learning via text messages. All of the schools liked the approach, were keen to continue and the project precipitated them towards thinking more broadly about vocabulary and book selection.

Practitioner Studies

All three studies are unpublished but provide small scale practitioner research in classroom contexts.

1 Emma Egan, teacher at Deanburn Primary School instigated a '30 words in 30 days' challenge for her P5 to 6 (9- to 10-year-olds). Emma used *Word Aware* approaches to directly teach one word per

day. She found the approach effective and on average the children moved from knowing three of the words at the start to knowing 26. The children's view of themselves as word learners also improved. Importantly, the use of the words in children's writing continued to rise even after the intervention had ceased.

2 Pamela Cummings, a teacher from Glasgow, used *Word Aware* approaches to teach science vocabulary and compared its impact to a non-fiction topic that was being taught at the same time, but where *Word Aware* was not used. The children learnt more words under the *Word Aware* approach, with the most noticeable impact on 'low attaining' children.

3 Sharon Dedman, a class teacher from Sutton in London, conducted some small-scale research in her Year 3 class (7- to 8-year-olds). She implemented the STAR elements and measured the impact on spoken vocabulary as well as literacy skills. The intervention period lasted for 12 weeks and she analysed three children's performances closely as well as using class data to track the whole class.

The three focus children's understanding of spoken vocabulary showed progress on the *British Picture Vocabulary Scales* (1997), but this did not reach significance. Results are summarised in Table 1.

Table 1: BPVS results

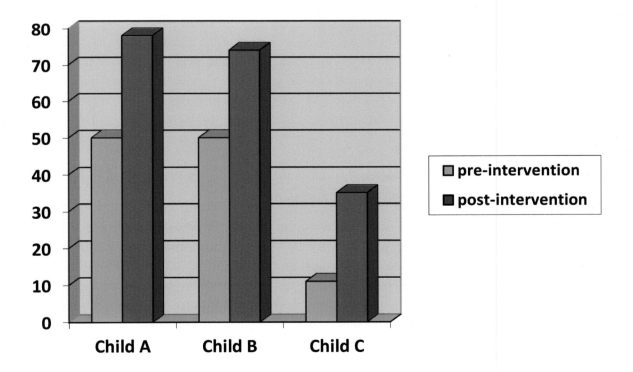

The three children's performance on the *Test of Word Finding* (German, 2000) did reach significance, indicating that their expressive vocabulary improved. Results are summarised in Table 2.

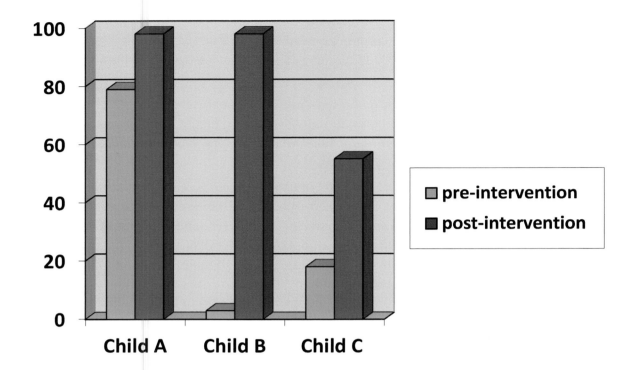

Table 2: Test of Word Finding

Sharon reported a positive impact on phonics and mixed impacts on reading and writing. This latter result may be because an improvement in spoken vocabulary is likely to take considerable time before it impacts on literacy. Sharon's general comments were that 'observations of the children indicated that they were definitely more interested in words and had become more curious about their meanings after implementing the programme's semantic word wall' (private communication).

Impact on School Data

The Aspire Educational Trust is a multi-academy trust of ten primary schools across the North West of England. They have been evaluating the impact of using *Word Aware*.

> The impact of this work has already been huge – some schools have been using the approach for a number of years and evidence can now be seen in data, other schools are earlier in their implementation but successful implementation is already being evidenced . . . Two schools who have been using the Word Aware approach for the past two years have seen positive results for their disadvantaged pupils, with them 'bucking the trend' and achieving above the standards achieved by non-disadvantaged pupils nationally.
>
> Jo Ashcroft. Director of Education at The Aspire Educational Trust,
> Aspirer Research School and Aspirer Teaching School.

Learning Along the Way

All of the studies listed here have focussed on direct teaching of words. Some have made an effort to also capture children's views, but at this point no studies have been conducted that investigate *Word Aware* in its entirety. Researching whole school change in a robust manner is a daunting task and beyond the scale of these projects.

However, even with limited time and budget it is still possible to investigate impact, but some general points on studying vocabulary interventions include:

- Be realistic and start small. Unless you have ring-fenced time, you will need to fit this around other duties and research takes time.

- Clearly define the intervention and outcomes. This is why STAR has been further researched than other aspects. It is comparatively easy to define and measure, but independent word learning strategies and getting children excited by words can also be specifically defined and measured.

- If others are delivering the intervention, ensure they are all trained and doing it correctly. Monitor and support as needed.

- If teaching specific vocabulary, change is much more likely to be captured on bespoke measures than on standardised measures, such as the BPVS (Dunn et al., 1997). Expressive vocabulary is more likely to respond than receptive.

- Impact on other areas will take even longer. Although research links vocabulary and reading development, there are few studies which show that improving vocabulary improves reading. This does not mean that change is not happening, but that it takes a long time for specific actions to have generalised effects.

- Reading comprehension has been a major focus for vocabulary research, but vocabulary also impacts on other areas of the curriculum, such as mathematics and science. Specific impact may be quicker in subject areas which have a more contained vocabulary.

- Look at qualitative measures such as student, parents and staff reports, interviews and questionnaires.

- Access support from universities. They do not necessarily need to be local, but will be of great help with design, data management and analysis.

- Data collection takes time, and so sampling a small number of children may be more manageable.

Assessing Direct Teaching of Vocabulary

The authors have conducted a number of small-scale audit-type projects focussed primarily on comparing direct teaching of words to a control set of words, which are still taught using 'regular' teaching. The control words are either in the same topic or in a different topic which is being taught at the same time. The results consistently showed that the direct teaching using *Word Aware* approaches does better than 'regular' teaching. A general summary of the process is provided below.

Purpose: To assess the impact of the STAR topic teaching method versus 'regular' vocabulary teaching.

Samples of six children per class are selected and their progress in topics in which STAR approaches are used is compared with topics in which no enhanced vocabulary teaching was done.

1. Select a topic in which to use the STAR approach and a topic from another subject that will be taught during the same period. This second topic will act as the control and no specific vocabulary teaching will be implemented.

2. For both topics, sort words into the 'anchor', 'Goldilocks' and 'step on' categories. Ensure you have a minimum of six Goldilocks words for each topic.

3. Select six children from the class who represent the diversity of word learners. For instance, two high, two intermediate and two low word learners should be selected. You may, of course, select the number you prefer, but beware that the data collection and analysis can be time-consuming.

4. Assess all 12 words using the method outlined below. Ideally this should be done by someone not directly involved with teaching this class.

5. Teach the six selected words over a number of weeks as outlined in Step 2.1, see page 152. The other six words are used in normal teaching but are not specifically taught.

6. Once the teaching period is complete repeat the assessment for all 12 words.

7. For extra robustness, the dates can be removed, numbering used instead of names, and the assessments mixed up and given to a third party to score. This reduces the likelihood of bias in the scoring.

8. Analyse the results comparing the intervention and the control words.

9. Feed back to senior school managers.

Assessing Vocabulary Knowledge
Instructions

1. Photocopy the Assessing Vocabulary Knowledge form (see page 329) for each selected child. Each child will be asked about vocabulary from each topic so you will need two sheets per child.

2. Individually ask each child about each of the 12 words (six for each topic). For every word, ask the children what they know about the word and to use it in a sentence. An example is provided on the next page.

4. Write down exactly what the child says. If they say little, then prompt them to say some more. DO NOT ask any further specific questions, as this may prompt them too much.

5. If the child defines an alternative meaning of the word (e. g.: if the relevant meaning of 'volume' related to capacity and the child described turning the 'volume' down on the TV), ask them if they know another meaning. Write down both answers.

6. After assessment, use the scoring guidelines given at the bottom of the Assessing Vocabulary Knowledge form to score the child's answer. Make a judgement about the child's overall knowledge of the word based on the combined responses to 'Tell me about the word' and 'Use the word in a sentence'. It is a judgement call, but it may be worth talking it through with a colleague to ensure consistency.

Assessing vocabulary knowledge

Word	Tell me what you know about the word	Use the word in a sentence	Overall score

Scoring guidelines

3 points	The student clearly understands the meaning of the word. The definition is clear and the word is used appropriately within a sentence. When viewed together the definition and the sentence show the student clearly understands the meaning of the word.
2 points	The answer indicates that the student has some understanding of the word but the listener has to infer some information. They may be able to use the word in a sentence appropriately but their definition is limited.
1 point	The student's definition or use of the word shows that it is possible that they have some understanding of the word. However, it is not clear that they do understand it. The listener needs to interpret the information.
0 points	The student is unable to give a description of the word's meaning or use it in an appropriate sentence. The student would score '0' if they describe another meaning of the word targeted and are unable to give the targeted meaning.

Assessing vocabulary knowledge – completed example

Word	Tell me what you know about the word	Use the word in a sentence	Overall score
carriage	It's what you sit in.	The carriage has a horse and a man.	2
harp	The harp makes noises.	The harp was making noises.	1
space	It's in space.	's-p-a-c-e'	0
midnight	It's really, really late.	At midnight it is very, very dark.	2
scroll	It tells you something. If you look somewhere like a church then somebody will read it to you.	If you are in a church, somebody will read it to you.	1
keyboard	A keyboard is on a computer. It has letters.	If you are typing some work, you press the keyboard.	3

References

Dunn, L. M., Dunn, D. M., Whetton, C. W. & Burley, J. (1997). *The British Picture Vocabulary Scale,* 2nd edition. Windsor: National Foundation for Educational Research.

German, D. J. (2000). *Test of Word Finding*, 2nd edition. Austin, TX: Pro-ed.

Herman, R., Hulme, C., Roy, P. & Kyle, F. E. (2020). A Pilot Study to Evaluate an Integrated Phonics and Language Programme for the Teaching of Reading to Deaf and Hearing Children https://openaccess.city.ac.uk/id/eprint/24046/1/

Moran, E. & Moir, J. (2018). Closing the vocabulary gap in early years: Is 'Word Aware' a possible approach? *Educational and Child Psychology*, 35, 51–64.

Web references

Jo Ashcroft's blog for Aspirer Research School: https://researchschool.org.uk/aspirer/news/an-evidence-based-approach-to-improving-oral-language-skills-of-disadvantaged-pupils/